Living On

Living On

A Study of Altering Consciousness After Death

Paul Beard

PILGRIM ⬤ BOOKS
TASBURGH NORWICH ENGLAND

First published in 1980
© George Allen & Unwin (Publishers) Ltd 1980
This edition © Paul Beard 1987

British Library Cataloguing in Publication Data
Beard, Paul
Living on.
1. Future life
I. Title
133.9'013   BF1311.F8
ISBN 0 946259 24 0

Reproduced and printed in Great Britain
at the University Printing House, Oxford
by David Stanford
Printer to the University

*To
Tony,
gratefully*

Author's Acknowledgements

I am greatly obliged to the College of Psychic Studies for kind permission to quote from various College of Psychic Studies Papers, and to Mrs Zöe Richmond for extracts from 'Joe's Scripts', published in *Light*, the Journal of the College of Psychic Studies. My thanks are due to the Society for Psychical Research and the Editor of its *Proceedings* for permission to publish extracts from Volume 33 of the Journal; I would like to make it clear that the S.P.R. holds no corporate views, and the opinions expressed in its publications are those of the authors alone.

Messrs Rider & Co. Ltd and the Hutchinson Publishing Group have shown special courtesy in allowing me to make quotations from Albert Pauchard's *The Other World*, both from the sections published in College of Psychic Studies Paper No. 7 and for the original book published by Rider & Co.; and for permitting me to quote from a symposium *Life, Death and Psychical Research*, *They Survive* by Geraldine Cummins, and *The Blue Island* by Woodman & Stead. Thanks are due to *The Observer* for permission to make a quotation on page 13 from an interview with Mr Graham Greene. I also thank Miss Rosamond Lehmann, who has kindly assented to the inclusion of an extract from her writings; and the Revd Charles Fryer for allowing me to quote, in advance of publication, from his work *A Hand in Dialogue*.

Thanks are due to the White Eagle Lodge Publishing Trust for several quotations, including material privately distributed, and also to Ivan Cooke and The White Eagle Lodge Publishing Trust for a quotation from *Thy Kingdom Come* by Ivan Cooke. Mr Maurice Barbanell of Psychic Press Ltd has generously permitted me to quote at will from the following Psychic Press publications: *As One Ghost to Another*, *The Road to Immortality*, *In the Dawn Beyond Death*, *The Shining Brother*, *The Betty Book*, *The Doorway*, *Beyond Life's Sunset* and *The Great Reality*.

I am also grateful to the publishers who have allowed me to quote from the undermentioned:

The Anthroposophical Press for *The Bridge over the River*; Basil Blackwell Ltd for a quotation from *Gate of Remembrance* by F. Bligh Bond; Cambridge University Press for *Something Beyond* by Revd A. F. Webling; the Churches' Fellowship for Psychical & Spiritual Studies, for passages from *Testimony of Light* by Helen Greaves, and *The Celtic*

Church Speaks Today by Revd A. W. Jackson; James Clarke & Co. for *The Interpretation of Cosmic and Mystical Experiences* by Dr R. Crookall; Collins Publishers for *Life Beyond Death with Evidence* by Revd Drayton Thomas; J. M. Dent & Sons for *The Mystical Element of Religion* by Baron von Hugel; Hodder & Stoughton for Dr Raynor C. Johnson's *Watcher on the Hills* and *The Spirit of the Hills* by F. S. Smythe; the Hogarth Press for *Jung and the story of our time* by Laurens van der Post; John Lane, the Bodley Head, for *Widening Horizons* and Constable & Co. for *Horizons of Immortality*, both by Baron Palmstierna; Longmans for *Personality Survives Death* by Lady Barrett; Mockingbird Books, USA, for *Life after Life* by Dr Raymond A. Moody, Jr; Mowbray for *Take it or Leave it* by Chancellor the Revd E. Garth Moore; Pelican Books for *The Personality of Man* by G. N. M. Tyrell; the Rosicrucian Fellowship, Mt Ecclesia, P.O. Box 713, Oceanside, California 92054 for Max Heindel's *The Rosicrucian Cosmo-Conception*; Routledge & Kegan Paul for extracts from *Swan on a Black Sea* by Geraldine Cummins; Neville Spearman for *Post-Mortem Journal* by Jane Sherwood; *The Awakening Letters* by Cynthia Sandys and Rosamond Lehmann, and *Private Dowding* by W. Tudor Pole; the Spiritualist Association of Great Britain for *Trance Talks* by Ivy Northage; the Student Christian Movement Press for *The Truth about Spiritualism* by Canon Harold Anson; Turnstone Books and Wildwood Press from *On the Death of my Son* by Jasper Swain; Watkins and the International Institute for *Discarnate Influence in Human Life* by Professor E. Bozzano.

I must ask for indulgence if I have overlooked or failed to trace any source from which permission to quote should have been sought, and in particular where it has not been possible to trace publishing firms which appear to be no longer extant.

Finally I acknowledge with pleasure my great debt of gratitude to Brenda Marshall for much patient work on, and valuable suggestions for, the text and for her unfailingly cheerful good will and moral support at all times.

Contents

Author's Acknowledgements

One thing I feel sure, if there is such a thing as life after death it won't be a static state. I think it will be a state of movement and activity. I can't believe in an ultimate happiness which doesn't include a form of development . . . A kind of evolution. Evolution of the spirit. And an eternity of evolution.

Graham Greene, in an interview with John Heilpern, *The Observer,* December 75.

In my end is my beginning.
(Last words of Mary Queen of Scots)

We have split up life into two parts far too drastically. We have drawn a line, and we must gradually erase that line. We have talked about the spiritual life and the earth life or the physical life. The two are one and we must make them one again . . . There is only one world and we must take down . . . these barriers of illusion that compelled us to think there must be two . . . It is your work, it is our work.

Oliver Lodge (posthumously)

PART ONE

Introduction

CHAPTER 1

A Case to Consider

1

What is it possible to discover about the experiences we shall meet with after we die – if indeed existence does continue – and about how we can best prepare for them?

If old friends were to return to us after death so changed that we failed to recognise their identity, then it would be impossible for them to convince us of their survival. We can conceive that such a change might come about, but then belief in survival could only be by faith and not from evidence. Therefore, faith apart, the effective case for a world into which men and women do enter after death depends first upon strong enough factual evidence to convince us that our own old friends still exist, that indeed we can and shall encounter them again. Plenty of such evidence exists, although different people give differing valuations to it. For those who find it convincing in general, this kind of evidence, however, is not enough. A good deal more is still required.

For to produce only memories of facts long past amounts to no more than what F. W. H. Myers has called 'wearisomely presenting his credentials'. What of his present life, into which he carries forward these memories? Memory cannot be limited to facts. Emotions, sometimes very strong ones, are also intertwined with it. If past facts can be remembered, the old emotions which accompanied them in the past may well continue too in the heart of the one who felt them. With new experiences after death, these emotions could change, grow, diminish. Life after death will hardly be worth calling life if it remains merely static. That is one reason why nobody believes any more in the playing of harps.

The evidence gains strength because it points to a process of development, one which starts from the recognisable self we brought from the old life on earth. It strongly suggests a principle of continuity. We ask whether this evidence shows that the dead are still sufficiently like their old selves for us to recognise them, yet different enough to convince us that they have undergone meaningful experiences since they left us, experiences which we in turn will face in due time. If their own reported words depict changes in their situation and in their own characters, whether for better or worse, these must be of an intelligible kind. They must persuade us that as well as a past they also possess an active present and a future, that their life is one which is worth living, that they are indeed something more than a mere memory bank.

This book attempts to assess the composite picture of post-mortem experiences as presented by the evidence which we so far possess.

2

Towards the close of his life Mozart wrote in his most intimate vein to his father :

Since death (properly understood) is the true ultimate purpose of our life I have for several years past made myself acquainted with this truest and best friend of mankind so that he has for me not only nothing terrifying any more but much that is tranquilising and consoling ! . . . death . . . [is] the key to our true blessedness.[1]

To speak thus at a dinner party today would invite stares and a rapid change of topic. Frank speech about death is uncomfortable. Unlike Mozart, many have not come to terms with it. If the picture we have of living on after death makes more sense than is commonly supposed then death may gradually cease to be the taboo subject of modern times.

In William Morris's *News from Nowhere*, the reader finds out that 'Nowhere' is a Utopia. The 'Nowhere' of life after death, as pictured in popular accounts, has an all-too-Utopian and unconvincing colouring.

However, when we search within a more serious context, we discover that the picture is somewhat different. The material need not be dismissed with a defensive wave of the hand as nonsense. For evidence does exist of a far more purposeful, strenuous and therefore rewarding kind of life, lived after death. We can collect the varying evidence as we would with any type of field evidence, and judge the similarities and differences in the accounts. I shall concentrate largely upon that part which seemingly emanates from witnesses who were of good calibre when on earth and whose accounts strongly suggest they retain this quality. Such accounts are by no means Utopian.

Modern depth psychology has produced a deepening picture of the human psyche and of powerful hidden forces it has discovered at work behind human emotions. Energetic fieldwork in the consulting room has brought about highly effective insights into traumas and into creative individuating patterns found over and over again.

[Jung] established in a way that no scientist can deny that this collective unconscious within man [and] the visions and dreams and imagery in which it communicated with man's conscious self were utterly objective facts, however subjectively they were experienced.[2]

Similar qualities of insight could well prove rewarding in what is at present regarded by psychical research as largely a subjective area. Surely it can be possible that in time, lying behind the personal accounts, objective patterns of post-mortem experience will gradually emerge.

For instance, it is now beyond dispute that the unconscious

finds ways of telling us things which have lain within our nature without our being aware of them, and which it then becomes important for the outer conscious self to learn to deal with. This often brings disclosures of arduous work which must be carried out to bring order both into the outer life and into the inner being or psyche. Sometimes it must come about that this psychological work remains unfinished, or not started, by the time death takes place. If then we continue as ourselves, inheriting our old character, we must expect to inherit our faults along with the rest. A legacy could then be brought from earth, a legacy of work upon the self unfinished there but which, unlike on earth, cannot subsequently be refused indefinitely. Alleged postmortem narratives describe a continuing therapy carried out by and upon the self through an intimate process of regeneration, a process which replaces old-fashioned and terrifying concepts of final judgement and punishment. We can then begin to ask, partly within the context of the expanding psychological world of modern man, what sort of meaningful causal relationship can exist between a person's life pattern on earth and the shape it is found to take after it.

Nor need death inevitably extinguish old relationships. They may continue in a new shape, springing from a change of heart towards a person left behind, and bringing altered feelings, as in Mrs Willett's posthumous letter to her son, quoted later in this chapter.

Another and wider element has also to be assessed. The accounts speak of teachers who exhibit a brotherly concern for their fellows recently arrived. Their insight, personal and impersonal, can perhaps also bear meanings relevant for those of us who remain on earth. It is worth examining.

Essentially, then, we shall be concerned with studying human values in a lifespan much extended by further experiences claimed to come about after death, and which, if true, could have very important relevances to our present life.

3

The picture we are to study is a mosaic made up of contributions both small and large. In Dr Robert Crookall's books alone – *The Supreme Adventure* and its companion volumes – will be found several hundred fragments of accounts of alleged discarnate experiences. My particular task is to seek contributions from post-mortem minds of good calibre. If a report were to appear of an unannounced arctic or tropical exploration we would examine it for internal coherence and then examine the reputation for truth and integrity of those who produced it. If people who on earth were of substance and integrity claim to send back after their death reports of what they have found, these are worthy of being read with special care. Those to whom the reports were addressed, and who express confidence in them, must expect to find their own integrity similarly scrutinised. This is perfectly fair.

I will now introduce some of the characters in whose name communications have since appeared, and who form the main cast of communicators in this book.

The volume and quality of psychical research carried out over the last hundred years by scientifically qualified minds is not yet generally recognised. It is too easily assumed that material which relates to posthumous communications is largely confined to the ramblings of uneducated mediums, and to listeners whose minds have been disturbed and made credulous by grief, with a consequent loss of all critical faculty. This is an erroneous and unrealistic view. The actual situation is otherwise.

This common opinion supposes that Sir Oliver Lodge, distracted by grief over the loss of his son Raymond in the First World War, allowed his emotions and his desire for comfort to overcome him and thus to bring about a conviction of survival which his unclouded scientific mind would never have reached. However, to examine his many contributions to the *Proceedings* of the Society for Psychical Research is to recognise that before he lost his son Oliver Lodge, with impressive scientific integrity, had spent thirty years in persistent and at times ingenious inquiry into communications claiming to be from discarnate sources. It took him a very long time to reach a working hypothesis of survival. As he said himself, the death of Raymond and the evidence he then received did not bring about his acceptance of survival, it merely confirmed for him the hypothesis which he had already reached from his many years of detached scientific labour in this field.

If communications claiming to be from Oliver Lodge show something of this same integrity, they will surely require to be looked at with care, irrespective of what any reader's final verdict may be. If Lodge survives, he will be particularly well qualified to produce material of significance. He is one member of our cast.

The next is the lady known as 'Mrs Willett', a pseudonym, her real name being Mrs Coombe Tennant. She was a J.P. and the first woman delegate from Britain to the League of Nations. The sensitive, mediumistic side of her life was kept very strictly private. Thus, Professor C. D. Broad, as a member of the Society for Psychical Research (and twice later to be its President), was familiar with her work, but although Mrs Coombe Tennant's son was his pupil at Trinity College, Cambridge, and he met her occasionally and also visited her London house, he had no clue that his acquaintance was the well-known 'Mrs Willett'.

Mrs Willett was one of a handful of highly educated non-professional sensitives who were members of a team which included a group of Cambridge scholars. Their work continued for a number of years, and allegedly some of these scholars continued it after their own deaths. Other sensitives included Mrs Verrall, a classical lecturer at Newnham, her daughter Mrs Helen Salter, and Mrs Holland, who lived mostly in India and sent communications from there. The Cambridge scholars included the philosopher Professor Henry Sidgwick; a classical scholar, Professor A. W. Verrall; Frederick W. H. Myers, the poet and psychical researcher; Professor Butcher, The Right Hon. Gerald Balfour, and Mrs Nora Sidgwick (the first Principal of Newnham College). Mrs Sidgwick's brother, Arthur Balfour, Prime Minister, O.M., and a President of the Society for Psychical Research, was the recipient of some of the most touching and intimate of these communications.

From this work which spanned many years there resulted the celebrated Cross-Correspondences, which form the best sustained and carefully recorded evidence we have of survival and continuing purpose after death. A central feature was the production of recondite classical allusions, some requiring specialised knowledge to unravel them. Another feature was an apparent attempt to overcome the theory that all material might be derived telepathically by the sensitive from the mind of the recipient, by an ingenious plan to give one fragment of a communication to one sensitive, another fragment to a second, in such a way that the connection between the two only made sense when the final part of the message was given through a third sensitive. Mrs Willett (if it is she) thus described the Cross-Correspondences after her death, writing through the hand of Geraldine Cummins:

> The . . . Case might be likened to an orchestra's perfect performance. The several communicators were scholars, whose intellects were married to imaginations that cherished an ideal image of scholarly perfection in the evidence . . . The investigators and the mediums had sufficient imagination to envisage the . . . objective of perfection. Thus deep called to deep in a unified desire. An orchestra must play as one if the performance is to reach towards perfection . . .[3]

Mrs Willett and Frederick Myers, the third member of our cast, are, if one can so put it, important post-mortem contributors to the material in this book. Helen Salter, of the Cross-Correspondences group, also contributes, though more briefly.

Frances Banks was for many years a nun in an Anglican teaching order in Africa. Comparatively late in her life she developed powers of extra-sensory perception. As there was no room intellectually in her order for the implications of this gift, she eventually left with the blessing of her superiors, returned to England and took a job teaching male prisoners in Maidstone gaol. She became an active member of The Churches' Fellowship for Psychical and Spiritual Studies. From the results of a questionnaire seeking psychic experiences, which she sent to several hundred Christian members, she wrote *Frontiers of Revelation*. A close friend of hers, Helen Greaves, is a non-professional sensitive; Frances Banks and Helen Greaves practised telepathy together in the hope that after Frances' death she would be able successfully to convey to Helen that she indeed survived and to describe her post-mortem experiences. The scripts Helen Greaves later received from her are recorded in her book *Testimony of Light*. Again we have a person of proven integrity and one, moreover, of deep piety and of mystical perception.

The Revd C. Drayton Thomas, a Methodist parson and a well-known and respected member of the Society for Psychical Research, contributed a number of papers to its *Proceedings*. With the help of Mrs Gladys Osborne Leonard a professional medium who for a number of years worked exclusively for the Society for Psychical Research, he was able to question his father, also a Methodist minister, and his sister, on the experiences they met with and how they reacted to them. He also received news of a number of former parishioners with whose characters he had been reasonably familiar.

T. E. Lawrence, that highly individual but difficult and unforthcoming figure, whose courage none could dispute, describes through the hand of Mrs Jane Sherwood the formidable difficulties which faced him after death, difficulties clearly related to events of his life on earth, though in an unexpected way. Albert Pauchard, an important contributor, was during his life President of the Metapsychical Society of Geneva, again a man of intelligence and probity, and very confident about the sort of experiences he expected would await him. These, however, turned out to be somewhat different from his expectations.

Other characters quoted more briefly include W. T. Stead, the humanitarian journalist; Father Tobe, a Roman Catholic priest; Sir William Barrett, F.R.S., one of the earliest members of the Society for Psychical Research; Thoreau; a Lieutenant-General (name given by communicator in full, but withheld from publication); and an unnamed Doctor of Divinity. The recipients include Frederick Lawrence, an ecclesiastical architect; Baron Palmstierna, a Swedish ambassador; Lady Barrett, Dean of the London School of Medicine for Women; Jasper Swain, a South African lawyer and magistrate; J. H. Remmers, an engineer; Dr Sherwood Eddy, an American scholar and author of thirty-five books on international, social and religious questions; Rosamond Lehmann, the novelist; Jelly d'Arànyi, the concert violinist, whose sister, Adila Fachiri, also a concert violinist, was the medium; and Brigadier R. C. Firebrace, who served as an interpreter between Stalin and Churchill.

4

Post-mortem accounts are often considered as no more than rosy wish-fulfilment narratives, as brightly coloured as a travel brochure. Some accounts are of this kind but, as has been said, quite a different picture emerges when more serious communications are examined. There is nothing rosy, for example, in the posthumous letter to one of her sons which 'Mrs Willett' wrote shortly after her death through another sensitive, Geraldine Cummins. Miss Cummins had never met this son. It records a very early post-mortem experience of a *change of heart*.

My dear, dear Alexander,
It is my urgent need to write to you on a private matter that concerns us two. I have a humiliating confession to make and must cast away all pride . . . I have been a witness of the film of memory, the record of my life . . . There are, as you may know, underground chambers of the mind . . . I have . . . had a dismaying revelation of one of them. I feel I must share it with you or in future I shall have no peace of mind . . .

The year before you were born . . . my little girl Daphne died. Then . . . came the lovely hope of another baby-girl to replace Daphne. Oh I was so bitterly disappointed when I learnt this happy dream was a deluding fancy . . . I repulsed my baby-son, visited my bitterness on his tiny innocent self. It was more in thought than in act. But at that very early age the babe is subconsciously acutely sensible of the mother's emotion towards himself . . . It produced in you a certain shyness and caution in regard to your apparently capricious mother. For later . . . I felt remorseful and went from one extreme to the other and became devoted . . . But it was too late. My tiny boy, just beginning to walk, was independent, withdrew from my kisses, rejected my impulsive, violent affection. He was deep down alarmed by it. So eventually that primitive mother became hurt and annoyed and turned away from him just when she might have won by her persistence and gentleness. Thus a psychological barrier began to grow up between us . . . I see now that fundamentally I was a possessive mother . . . You, a sturdy little boy, refused to be owned . . . Quite often I have thought evilly of you . . . because you were completely independent of me . . . I have even in these posthumous messages written, I believe, false things about you. But these were all derived from my baffled emotional vanity because I failed in any sense to possess you. In this life when studying our past memories we assume the mood of the time in which these memories were happening. So I beg of you to remove from your mind any cruel, false thing I wrote of you in a posthumous message . . . Mine has been the initial offence all along. If you have felt a barrier between us, I created it not you. For the sake of my peace of mind I beg of you to forgive my grievous fault . . . Dear sons, I send you from the hither world my true love in equal shares.[4]

Do these strike the reader as indeed the words of a woman who after her death has undergone a real experience, a change of perspective which requires her to set old emotions right?

5

Let us take a bird's-eye view of the material we shall examine. It contains a good deal of variety. There are many stories of immediate arrival into the post-mortem situation. A good number tell of new surroundings; these are discovered later on to be partly conditioned by the survivor's own mental and emotional states. Such suroundings are not necessarily what they first appear to be. They have illusory elements. There is a wide variety of difficulties and of adjustments.

Post-mortem values have very little to do with earth reputation or achievement, nor are they always speedily discovered. Persons well known on earth, T. E. Lawrence for example, do not always get on well.

These travellers gradually extricate themselves from their difficulties, with help, but fundamentally by their own efforts. We see various ways in which, meanwhile, some remain entangled in the same problems they failed to deal with when on earth. In time a self-judgement arises of all the events of the past life and the result is sometimes painful. With adjustment to this new life, the mental and emotional powers gradually become keener and deeper, but the resulting growth and change in values calls for a good deal of strenuous effort. Ethical and spiritual laws are found to govern life after death, but these do not fully coincide with those given in conventional religious teaching on earth.

Many accounts picture how human beings come to revalue the various aspects of their own character. They reorient themselves, too, to changes in the nature of human relationships. Meetings are described with superior intelligences who, it becomes evident, have little interest in what we would call their own personality. Companionship alters and intensifies. As such changes come about, narrators proclaim that they are finding that life is much larger than foreseen by them on earth, and yet they recognise that they are still only at the very beginning of knowledge.

6

It is not an easy task to assess the pictures of postmortem existence claimed to be given by men and women actually living it.
The reader is not expected to share my assumptions, to accept
the narratives, or my interpretations, or the existence of the
communicators themselves. It would be tedious in the extreme,
however, if intellectual reserves and qualifications were added on
every page. The reader if he wishes can add his own. My intention is to report with as faithful an understanding as I can
muster what these narratives, taking one with another, are
attempting to tell us, and then to leave the reader to form his
own judgements.

Before commencing to sift the evidence, we must take a look
in the next chapters at some fundamental problems it raises for
us. How strong has psychical research so far found the evidence
for survival itself? As for the experiences described as taking
place subsequently, can a sound methodology be found to assess
such elusive material? What confidence can be felt in its sources?
How reliable can we judge them to be? And some persons will
wish to ask in particular : it is morally justified to approach the
material at all?

Readers, however, who prefer to proceed straight to the
narratives can turn to Chapter 5, omitting Chapters 2–4, or
reading them after the rest of the book.

CHAPTER 2

Psychical Research and Survival

For a hundred years and more psychical research has rigorously investigated the evidence for survival of death, and the nature of the faculty which produces it. How far has it reached? The position now is one where theoretical difficulties delay – some think delay unduly – the setting up of any working hypothesis, whether it be one which is favourable or unfavourable to survival.

Properly recorded evidence exists in plenty. Some of it is very cogent. It has been studied in many books, some for the researcher, others for the general reader.[1] It is not my purpose to retell it here. It is also open to any layman to seek his own private evidence.

Since the subject has been actively investigated by a sufficient number of scientists as well as by many other intellectually disciplined people over this long period, one could reasonably expect that the evidence would long since have become established, or else been discredited. All this time savants have approached the material confidently expecting that it would all be explained away in one way or another as derived from other available sources of information, or from malobservation, maldescription or fraud. But all has not been thus explained away. A good deal of the evidence remains intact. Yet it continues to present the same problems of acceptance. Where then does the difficulty lie?

The reason is that unfortunately we still know virtually nothing of the *mode* of operation of the extra-sensory faculty which brings the evidence to us. Therefore scientists have been unable to create a paradigm or framework within which it can be understood. Until they can, some do not accept the existence of ESP as factual. They consider it wiser to regard it as not yet established. A further difficulty is that its sporadic nature makes it hard to test. It cannot readily be produced at will. Moreover, those who exhibit it often cannot tell whether they are functioning accurately. What they say can sometimes prove to be incorrect when they are most certain it is true.

If they can thus be shown to be unreliable in reporting telepathy from persons on earth, this lessens for many scientists the credibility of any claim that ESP can place them also in mental touch with persons who have survived death. It does not of course disprove it. Nor do the errors overturn startlingly correct facts which strongly suggest a source in discarnate minds. It is for scientists to account for this accurate material in other ways if they can.

A few set up a theory that we are reduced after death to a fading memory bank (some call this a psychon) from which ESP draws this material. This implies that we suffer a shadelike diminishing epilogue with no new features in it, no fresh nourishment from past or present. Those who favour this theory offer no explanation of how such a psychon exists, nor is it clear how far a psychon is held to be aware of itself. The theory cannot satisfactorily account for much of the material.

Many scientists resist acceptance of a survival hypothesis because the well established framework of productive scientific observation, research, and predictable and repeatable experiments in other fields seems to them to make survival most unlikely to be a fact. Survival also goes against the philosophical implications of scientific materialism.

Therefore many take the stand that probability, as well as Occam's Law of the minimum hypothesis, call upon them to prefer for the time being any other explanation as more likely than that of survival. This produces difficulties in believing favourable evidence gathered by former scientists. They will not build upon their work. It is much easier to conclude that they were deceived or deceived themselves. Against this viewpoint, a

✶ SEE DICIONARY RE: OCKANT'S RAZOR

number of other scientists consider that the evidence is strong, and justifies or requires a working hypothesis that we do survive death. There is no uniformity of scientific opinion on the subject. This division results in something of an impasse.

Let us take a brief look at the inherent evidential difficulties. A sensitive or medium presents facts which are seemingly unknown to the recipient. The sceptic will object that the facts, even if not present in the conscious mind, could formerly have been known, remaining stored in the recipient's memory though he cannot recall them. He will say that it is from there that the extra-sensory perception of the sensitive somehow dredges them up. However, if this is so, then the process by which the facts are thus gained remains still entirely unknown.

On the other hand, if facts are produced which as far as can be ascertained never had been known to the recipient, then it becomes necessary to verify them either by reference to some document – a letter or a written record – or else through the memory of some other living person. The sceptic then suggests two possibilities. The first is that the sensitive's ESP somehow has mysterious access to the document, wherever it is kept, and can read it however closely it is folded. Or else he says that the material is filched from the living mind of the person who can consciously remember it, even though this person and his whereabouts are and always have been totally unknown to the sensitive.

If some other theory is preferred to that of deliberate communication from the person now dead, such a theory must involve remarkable powers – wide-ranging and instantly available – of gaining possession of facts from unknown minds or distant places. This is called super-ESP to distinguish it from ESP which either draws its material from the recipient present at a seance, or apparently receives it spontaneously from a discarnate mind.

We then face a difficulty about super-ESP, well expressed by the posthumous F. W. H. Myers. He pointedly asks: 'Who selects?' How does the sensitive know the right mind or the right document to rifle, and, sitting in a chair, instantly read it at a distance?

The battlefield in the survival issue therefore does not lie in the evidence, which is ample, but in interpreting its source. If a working hypothesis favouring survival is rejected, this then requires a theory of super-ESP of such staggering range and accuracy that it would be unreasonable to attribute it to any human being. The exponent of super-ESP needs to ask himself how unlikely are the facts he has to posit. If he seriously holds that sensitives do have these super-powers, then he must test them. But this sort of fieldwork does not seem to interest the psychical researcher. The theory of super-ESP must be classed at present as little more than a defensive sceptical device.

If a working hypothesis of survival is to be avoided it necessitates this theory of such extreme complication that it has not been experimentally tested as an alternative and probably cannot be.

The issue of survival after death is most unlikely to be settled by the arrival of some knock-down cases. In the current intellectual climate cold winds continue to blow against it, creating an unfavourable environment for consideration of the direct evidence. As long as we do not know the limits of the human mind – and we never shall – it will doubtless be possible to devise ingenious alternative theories which can then all too readily be left unproven. The issue is more likely to be solved in other ways. Many more persons than at present may find the way to ESP experiences of their own, thus providing their own direct evidence. Much will depend too on whether or not the cumulative evidence of effective, meaningful discarnate communication becomes more and more weighty, or less and less so, as experience grows and experiment continues. It needs combined operations by the many who care passionately, on behalf of truth, where – if anywhere – human destiny leads us after death.

CHAPTER 3

Problems of Assessment and Acceptance

1

Common human attitudes towards death, and the taboos which surround it, often impede a direct personal examination of the material. There can be intellectual, emotional or religious obstacles. Many people do not find it easy to overcome them, or to breach the near-conspiracy of social silence about death. Other, different, obstacles inhere within the material; make it difficult to assess, and add to the distrust which many feel. Thus there can be a deeply entrenched distrust present in many before the start.

2

Fear of death is a compound emotion. One may postpone thinking of death as one postpones making one's will. If one holds it to be impossible to survive physical death, the subject becomes painful as well as fruitless; most painful of all when one is brought to face the extinction of those deeply dear. There is fear of the unknown, whether it be extinction or the reverse. There is fear of the pain expected to precede and accompany the experience. There is, too, a fear of moral consequences which could arise if there is survival, of finding a code that one has failed to live up to, leading to remorse, punishment, or self-punishment.

On the other hand it can be a real relief to think of oblivion bringing cessation to a tired and failing body. The struggle with life's problems can be diminished or dismissed, too, if one believes concern with them will last for so short a while. Yet whenever extinction is anticipated, whether with stoicism, with desire or with relief, there is also likely to be one part of us which, despite intellectual conviction, does nevertheless hope and long for continuation of some sort, a part which a man sometimes represses or scorns or deals with harshly.

There is, too, a different kind of fear which arises out of allegiance to religious teachings. It is natural and indeed proper, before examining so highly important a theme, to feel anxiety lest one becomes deceived, and to suspect the trustworthiness of the sources.

Therefore, overall, there is a noticeable gap in modern man's curiosity about what may await us all after death, the more singular since death is inevitable. This gap is the oddest of omissions in our otherwise insatiable thirst for knowledge. It is especially curious since life, if it continues, could prove to be for a period enormously longer than our few years on earth.

3

The basic concept that we live on after death has also to face the formidable school of medical opinion which postulates that consciousness cannot be conceived of without the physical body which is regarded as its essential vehicle of expression, and that therefore life after death is impossible. True, this view is not unanimous; another weighty neurological school conceives mind as distinct from the brain which forms its vehicle. Perhaps for a long time ahead it will remain possible as it is today to argue a case for either position. If from investigation in other fields the evidence for survival of death is held to be strong enough, some will expect this to settle the matter for neurologists too, on the grounds that it will independently establish continuation of consciousness without and apart from the physical body. It is not likely to settle it, however, for this is not the direction to which neurologists turn their main attention. They rely on the evidence which their own expertise best qualifies them to interpret, on what their studies of the physical body appear to tell them.

4

I once told a friend I was writing about the post-mortem world. He asked with a twinkle: 'Have *you* been there?' An inescapable factor in the testimony is that it has to be of a hearsay kind. By definition it deals with experiences we cannot yet have whilst we are on earth, or at least not in the way in which the dead know them. The facts are not on earth. We have to work within this clear methodological limitation. This drawback of hearsay, though inevitable, is disagreeable to many precise minds. As we have seen, many psychical researchers therefore prefer to ignore the accounts as having no place in strict research. They cannot find a way to measure them. The mode of production of the evidence, too – whatever the method by which it can be conceived as being introduced or intruded into minds living on earth – can clearly be suspect. Many would expect the material to be a mere projection based on the psychological needs of its producer. Or it could be no more than something that those who write the material down consider to be likely. They could be imagining it all.

Now either the material, or some of it, has its source in discarnate minds, or else it has not. If we do not survive, the accounts must be false. If we do survive but no communication is possible, then in theory some things in the accounts might be correct by coincidence. No one will examine the accounts on this ground. If we do survive and some degree of communication is possible, then we have to try and sort out what is real and what unreal in the material. It is not difficult to detect material which is no more than an exercise for the writer's wish-fulfilment, or which all revolves around him and feeds his ego, or which merely reflects earlier writings by other people. Such pseudo-accounts are easy to dismiss.

When accounts are serious in tone and appear to attempt to present information honestly, more difficult problems of judgement arise.

5

The human mind likes to demand certainty, but in most matters we expect and rely upon degrees of probability. Science is built on observations and deductions which later become probabilities. At any time a number of its current working hypotheses are likely to be discounted after further investigation. The history of science is strewn with discarded hypotheses.

Similarly, in the field we are going to study, if we come to accept some of the material as bona fide we must expect only a provisional picture. Parts of the evidence accepted by students today can, like scientific hypotheses, be superseded later. More skilful communicators and more accurately attuned sensitives may produce better material. Total certainty, whether scientific, philosophical, theological or revelatory, must not be looked for. It would be an illusion to look for it.

Michelangelo's Sistine ceiling depicts Adam's arm stretched out towards God, able to touch no more than the tip of His finger. If discarnates can reach us, it must needs be (speaking figuratively) by an equally slender touch from their still human fingers. We are judging human testimony, with all its imperfections. Obviously problems arise of the reliability of communicators, and also of accurate reception of what is transmitted.

We come to see very soon that no post-mortem communication emerges entirely in the shape in which it was intended to be given. For the sensitive who receives the material also has insensitivities as well as prejudices and limitations of perception, causing the material to become coloured, altered or diluted by passage through his or her mind. This is unavoidable.

Because the material alike by its nature and the roundabout process by which it has to reach us is condemned to imperfection, this does not deny it validity. If a man does survive and wants to tell of it, how else can he do it except through the limited instrument of human beings still on earth? Some sort of compromise there has to be between requirements of precision, on our side, and the difficulties which communicators, if genuine, will face in finding expression. It requires a certain tolerance towards their attempts to get round the obstacles that we come to see must exist for them. Too rigorous a methodology would lead to excluding material which though imprecise can have meaning and which may point to genuine experiences. Unpalatable though it is, whatever methodology we devise must pay heed to these limitations.

6

The methodological problem is therefore one of credence: how far is credence legitimate, or how far does it expose us to an unjustifiable assent, perilously poised above a rapid descent to mere credulity? On the other hand how can we advance except by steps which have to be somewhat in the dark? In these difficult yet unavoidable circumstances where is the solid ground on which we can stand?

Coleridge in his famous dictum on poetry speaks of a willing suspension of disbelief. In our quite different field, advantage can result if with great care and caution we adopt this attitude towards what communicators seem to be trying to tell us. Let us examine Coleridge's three words separately. As long as the suspension is *willing,* it stays under our command, free from any emotional compulsion to accept. It needs to be a *suspension* and not an abandonment, because this leaves freedom to resume or assume disbelief if the material fails to satisfy us. And it will be necessary for *disbelief* to be put on one side temporarily, to allow the material to make its own unimpeded impact.

We are then able to be receptive in every area of our being. In poetry this is readily seen to be necessary. We do not dictate beforehand to the poet, but judge by the response he elicits. Like poetry, the material has the right to its own statements and meanings, yet it is also an attempt to communicate from one human being to another. Unfortunately the precision of words which illumines poetry is missing.

If we first allow full opportunity for communication on its own terms, and after that judge the material at the bar of *all* our human faculties, a methodological justification is reached.

A rounded picture cannot result if only part of our armoury of perceptual tools is used. Many criteria need to take their turn : reason, sensibility, imagination, the aesthetic sense; the whole equipment of man's many-sided being must be brought into the judgement. An intellectual, let us say, does not wish to be misled by his feelings. But feelings can lead as well as mislead. Intellect is invaluable in detecting inconsistencies and ambiguities which emotion ignores or even encourages. Yet emotion and intellect can both be highly resistant in this heavily charged field, clouded for many by fear and prejudice. Hence the need for a preliminary suspension of disbelief to make the way clear for the whole field of subsequent value judgements. At times they will compete with one another and perhaps seem contradictory, but surely putting them all to work will best enable the true picture gradually to emerge.

7

Whether we expect to survive it or not, death is usually regarded as a highly decisive event. This is partly why many turn their eyes away from it. However, it is a very large assumption that death, if we survive it, will bring any kind of final knowledge to us. According to reports, death certainly does not reveal all; it is only a stepping-stone to a long new chapter of experience. If an Aborigine were dropped by parachute into the centre of London, his powers of understanding what is now around him would be very circumscribed. His past life would be hampering him. Like the Aborigine, a communicator fairly soon after his death is likely to interpret what he sees in terms of already familiar earth facts, and before he has adjusted himself to its real nature. Meaning as on earth needs to be bought by experience. Fifty or a hundred years after their death, some survivors may know little more than when they first arrived. They can remain timid or blinkered. As on earth, some are likely to be eager students, but others laggards. One must attempt to distinguish good witnesses who have learned from bad ones who have not.

8

Three main difficulties are apparent in the production and transmission of post-mortem material.

The first difficulty arises when something needs to be described which does not exist on earth or is different from what it is on earth. This is primarily a difficulty of language. If post-mortem conditions turn out to be considerably different, it will be extremely hard for any communicator to find earth words to describe these as they really are. On the other hand, if they are presented in terms of earth similes, then the picture is bound to seem too much like a reproduction of earth existence, and unconvincing on that account. The familiar can be dismissed by the unwilling mind because it is familiar, and the unfamiliar on the grounds that it cannot be understood. Some things may be so unfamiliar as to defy description at all; discarnate accounts often say so. Unfortunately, one consequence of dying is that one loses thereby some of one's credibility as a witness.

Communicators themselves sometimes speak of their near-despair at their inability to convey more than a fragment of their intended meaning. Confronted with some factor which any possible description is bound to falsify, they are faced with the choice of accepting the falsity or else of not speaking of it at all. This could be a hard choice. It is evident that they sometimes exercise a necessary element of selection.

It is clearly sounder then if we give too little authority rather than too much to the accounts. Except for novices, discarnate communicators themselves are very seldom dogmatic. If they have learned to be so, it will be wise for us to be so similarly. No serious account will be found to claim that discarnate information is always full and accurate.

The second difficulty arises if, as a result of his experience, perhaps a lengthy one, the communicator has reached some altered state of consciousness, which can be hard for us to grasp and harder still, or impossible, to accommodate within our present thinking. To understand fully one would need to be both willing and able to change something in one's own consciousness. If the communicator considers this presents too hard a challenge, then he will be obliged to speak from something less than his full self; he may even have to appear, in order to reach us, as more like his former self than he now really is.

If the evidence gradually comes to suggest, as it does to some students, that beyond these personally known predecessors other wiser and more senior communicators also occasionally speak, then these too are likely to be obliged during communication to discard part of the total landscape of their knowledge. They will need to transform their consciousness down to a level at which we can understand it. It is not unlike the way in which we reduce part of our adult self when talking to a child. It would seem there has to be a kind of stepping-down process. The communicator has to tell us in terms of what he thinks we can understand. The sensitive, as has been said, in reporting the meaning can readily translate it in a faulty way and we, as recipients, will often find it much easier to reduce it further to familiar earth notions, to slot it into ways in which we are used to thinking rather than to stretch the mind towards more expanded concepts.

Thus to the first difficulty of material unfamiliar to us, and the second difficulty of speaking of and from a changed consciousness, there has to be added the third difficulty of successfully linking telepathically with the sensitive. It is easy to suppose this is a simple relaying or repeating of words, but everything suggests that it is nothing like so simple. The process is more like making another mind think the thoughts which are the communicator's own. Apart from the difficulty of receiving them and understanding them, how often is not the sensitive's thinking and feeling going to insist on its own way, and then pass this on in good faith as the communicator's own? The sensitive is essential if the message is to reach earth at all, and yet at the same time is the main obstacle the communicator has to try and circumvent.

The hostile critic can of course choose to declare *a priori* that all these are no more than excuses for a sensitive's own ineffective fabrications, but hostile critics do not necessarily examine all parts of the picture, and this is an area which still calls for a good deal of patient observation.

9

Survival after death does not in itself establish that life has meaning, although it certainly makes it infinitely more probable. Do the accounts show *a world worth living in*? If the picture bears no relation whatsoever to earth life with all its horrors and injustices and unfulfilments, this would offend logic. We urgently ask whether these pictures of following life contain an explanation, however partial and incomplete, of some of the mysteries which lie in this one. Hearing how others have fared after death can also hold implications for our own present. The behaviour of discarnates when they were still on earth very likely much resembled our own. Their present experiences therefore may well anticipate our own future. This in turn can suggest actions which, if taken by us on earth, will alter our own aftermath. For the aftermath must surely bear a logical relation to what has gone before, and vice versa. Act Two of the play, as it is gradually described after death, can make Act One more intelligible whilst we are engaged in playing it out on earth, and can begin to answer questions which arise from it; and it can give a promise of Acts Three, Four and Five to follow, as well as helping us to rewrite our private part of Act One whilst we are still on earth to do so.

10

In any life process, to learn involves an ability to change. If after death we survive but in no way alter, then there is no point in pursuing this inquiry, since it would imply that there is nothing more to be learned than we can already learn from earth. It is heartening to our inquiry to find, as we do, that everything points to those who have died having to feel their way gradually into the life they find around them, that man finds himself still engaged in a process of continuous learning. To learn is the purpose of many of his experiences there, as on earth. It is a continuation of the human adventure. Hence narrators will not all be recounting identical events. Therefore something more will be required than a literal comparison of accounts. The truth will certainly not be found by supposing that disagreement between them implies either that one is right and the other wrong, or alternatively that neither can be relied upon. If accounts arise from quite different levels of experience, clearly there is not and cannot be a flat equality in the testimony; it is a composite picture.

Respect for the accounts increases, however, when, even with their differences, they are seen after comparison to hang together reasonably well. Some parts certainly make a great deal of sense. When the witnesses do disagree with one another, the impression frequently arises that most witnesses are at least *trying* to tell the truth, even when we can see that their perceptions are limited.

The pictures thus show that it is essential to allow for a hierarchy of perception. Indeed, they imply that growth in consciousness is itself the key which gives access to further environments there without which entry remains barred, or self-barred. It is indicated that people can travel only as far as their spiritual stature allows.

Under these somewhat elusive conditions, the problem arises then of how to find a way to compare like with like. I have already pointed to an area where we are on comparatively firm ground. When we ask if we survive, we really mean: do we survive still as human beings, however much or little, however slowly or swiftly, we become changed? Whatever problems arise in trying to understand post-mortem environments or altered physical or non-physical make-up, the true line of continuity is between humans still talking to one another in terms of fellow feelings and thoughts. Again we are brought back to human testimony, and to grounds for its authenticity and veracity. This is the solid core on which we can best and most safely build in terms of value judgments.

11

Let us hypothetically divide our present nature into three aspects:

1   The everyday physical part which is at home on earth.
2   A part of us which, if we survive, will presumably find and learn how to be at home where the physical, at least as we know it here, is non-existent.
3   If (2) exists, then man on earth will be a compound, partly composed of his earthly self and partly of his continuing self, and there is likely to be somewhere within consciousness an area where the two overlap.

Is it a legitimate assumption that within some part of ourselves we shall find an answering echo to whatever is true in what we are told about life after death? The information should be akin to this part of our nature.

It is being increasingly recognised that in many parts of the scientific picture the observer is part of his observation; his tools of observation are not all strictly objective ones, but include the tool of his own mind. Professor Michael Polanyi writes at length of tacit knowing in man, apprehending tools which he has at his disposal and which give him many of his best raw materials.

He then needs, says Polanyi, to bring these down into his consciousness and assimilate them.

Perhaps a comparison with the well-known difficulty of communicating mystical experiences can be useful here. These can only be inadequately reported because they lie beyond the language of common experience. Not enough of us have as yet shared them. Yet in very different cultures they have a remarkable and convincing uniformity. They all bring about an enlargement of being and an absolute conviction of the ultimate goodness of the universe. (A factor of many of them, incidentally, is that all fear of death entirely vanishes.) When the mystical flash comes, it brings an instantly expanded level of consciousness which possibly the majority of men and women will reach only as the result of a long and strenuous sojourn in the realms beyond death. Mystics may thus anticipate what we shall all one day know. Some events of consciousness which will be quoted later from discarnate accounts resemble early steps on earth up this mystical ladder. Survival accounts and mystical accounts, however unequal in depth, can be seen as bringing support to one another. Parts of discarnate experience overlap with peak experiences on earth.

12

To judge whether the material is veridical, a mixed bag of canons is therefore needed. Here are some :

1   Is there an internal logic in what travellers tell us befalls them, leading the student to suppose that the world after death is an orderly one, even though its full order be difficult to discover ?

2   Behaviour as described will be more convincing the wider the range of humanity it covers. We need to know what happens to all sorts of people and not merely those congenial to the inquirer. The Christian inquirer, for instance, needs to listen to what non-Christians tell us, as well as to Christians.

3 Do accounts, though from speakers of different earth beliefs, still generally correspond with one another, as well as having reasonable areas of divergence? Are there also direct contradictions? If so, how far are they due to different levels of insight and experience? Can what is said to be true at one level of consciousness be compared with and perhaps replaced by a deeper view from beings of wider vision? In short, what evidence is there of many types of consciousness at work, depending on experience well earned through length of sojourn?

4 Are causal forces, whether benevolent or the reverse, seen more clearly at work in a further existence than in this strange world of our own? Is anything said of conflict there between good and evil?

5 In studying, do we find an inner recognition springing up within us of the truth of the descriptions? Are communicators educating us, in Platonic manner, towards something of which in one part of our beings we already have knowledge?

6 Can the after-death experiences recorded be utilised, and bear good fruit for those of us still on earth? Communicators from time to time suggest how to live better, declaring that what they have found in discarnate life applies just as much to us here and now. If, therefore, some of these suggestions are lived out with harmonious results, this could provide an indirect testimony of the material's validity.

7 Is there evidence of continuing direct relationships with those on earth helping, hindering or otherwise influencing present thoughts and actions? Telepathic help for, and continuing interest in, people on earth could turn out to be just as much a part of discarnate life as experience taking place solely within its own environment.

8 What is the nature of personal relationships in the post-mortem world? How far do spiritual relationships, and passionately loving ones, and family ties and occupational relationships continue or perhaps change in importance?

9 Above all, is there any acceptable picture of a Jacob's

ladder of consciousness dependent upon our own efforts
and not automatically bestowed upon us?

However approximate and incomplete, we shall hope to find
a degree of information on these important topics woven within
the texture of the accounts we shall be studying.

To summarise, we have seen that a general and widely spread
scepticism still remains towards accounts of life after death, and
that this is due to a variety of reasons: to the necessary limitations of the testimony as being only hearsay; to fear and suspi-
cion of its sources in sensitives and people in unusual states of
consciousness; to the difficulties which arise from the somewhat
fragmentary nature of the material; and to the lack as yet of a
scientifically acceptable paradigm. Yet it is necessary and
honourable to give fair hearing to what could prove to be valid
human testimony on matters of the deepest import to mankind.
Whatever methodological approach is chosen, this requirement
needs to be satisfied.

Do these voices, then, awaken response from our private sense
of reality and deepen it? Do they introduce to us a different and
more widely involved logic of consequence? Are they sufficiently
keenly expressive to convince us that here are indeed human
beings speaking to us from a different area of consciousness, but
one in which they still react in a recognisable way as we might
expect ourselves to react? Are some accounts only a tale told
by an idiot? Are some told by wise individuals, and are others
honest accounts of experiences, recounted at times joyfully, at
times ruefully, by one's peers?

Let us next take a look at the sources of this information,
and ask how reliable we can expect them to be.

CHAPTER 4

The Sources

1

How far then can we trust the sources and the integrity of those who provide them? The main contribution, of course, lies in telepathic communications claimed to be from men and women on the further side of death. This method provides us with the most varied information at present available. The witnesses, however, are necessarily absent and cannot be extradited for personal cross-examination. Provided they are not mere figments, there is one advantage in their being absent. They are surely in a better position than we are to obtain information, although in a worse position to communicate it. At first sight this difficulty of absence can be bypassed if persons still on earth can gain glimpses for themselves into the world after death, at least to a degree.

This is claimed to be possible in two ways.

2

The first is based on the witness of some persons who, irrespective of age, have lain near death, or have momentarily been clinically dead, and who have then found themselves in an externalised form of consciousness, often seemingly from a point from where they have observed their physical body lying on the bed. They appear to enter or at least to glimpse a new environment and talk to discarnate persons. On their recovery to normal health they describe these experiences, which usually have, and continue to have, a profound effect on them. These 'brief glimpse' accounts – Peak in Darien cases as F. W. H. Myers called them – have a considerable measure of agreement with one another, though of course they are not uniform. The following contains features present in many accounts.

> . . . I rapidly became very ill and I felt much worse. I was lying in bed, and I remember trying to reach over to my wife and say that I was very sick, but I found it impossible to move. Beyond that, I found myself in a completely black void, and my whole life . . . flashed in front of me . . . I went from grammar school to high school to college, then to dental school, and then right on into practising dentistry.
>
> I knew I was dying, and I remember thinking that I wanted to provide for my family. I was distraught that I was dying and yet that there were certain things that I had done in my life that I regretted, and other things that I regretted that I had left undone.
>
> The flashback was in the form of mental pictures . . . but they were much more vivid than normal ones. I saw only the high points, but it was so rapid it was like looking through a volume of my entire life and being able to do it within seconds. It just flashed before me like a motion picture that goes tremendously fast, yet I was fully able to see it, and able to comprehend it. Still, the emotions didn't come back with the pictures, because there wasn't enough time.
>
> I didn't see anything else during this experience. There was just blackness, except for the images I saw. Yet I definitely felt the presence of a very powerful, completely loving being there with me all through this experience.[1]

Some accounts describe separation of consciousness. The following case was vouched for by Sir Auckland Geddes:

> I realised that *my* consciousness was separating from another consciousness which was also me. These we could call the A- and B-consciousnesses, and throughout what follows, the

ego attached itself to the A-consciousness . . . I realised that the B-consciousness belonging to the body was beginning to show signs of being composite – that is, built up of 'consciousness' from the head, the heart and the viscera. These components became more individual and the B-consciousness began to disintegrate, while the A-consciousness, which was now me, seemed to be altogether outside my body, which it could see. Gradually I realised that I could see, not only my body and the bed in which it was, but everything in the whole house and garden, and then realised that I was seeing not only 'things' at home but in London and in Scotland, in fact wherever my attention was directed; . . . and the explanation which I received, from what source I do not know, but which I found myself calling to myself my mentor, was that I was free in a time-dimension of space, wherein 'now' was in some way equivalent to 'here' in the ordinary three-dimensional space of everyday life.[2]

The next example did not arise in illness but in the prime of physical fitness. A fall occurred to the well-known Himalayan mountaineer, F. S. Smythe:

. . . Though I had assumed . . . that I was as good as dead, I made desperate attempts to stop myself . . . During the time that I was doing this, a curious rigidity or tension gripped my whole mental and physical being. So great was this tension that it swamped all pain and fear, and rendered me insensible to bumps and blows. It was an overwhelming sensation, and quite outside my experience. It was as though all life's forces were in process of undergoing some fundamental evolutionary change, the change called death, which is normally beyond imagination and outside the range of ordinary human force or power . . . I know now that death is not to be feared, it is a supreme experience, the climax, not the anti-climax, of life.

For how long I experienced this crescendo of power I cannot say. Time no longer existed as time; it was replaced by a sequence of events from which time as a quantity or quality in terms of human consciousness no longer existed. Then, suddenly, this feeling was superseded by a feeling of complete indifference and detachment, indifference to what happened

to my body, detachment from what was happening or likely
to happen to that body. I seemed to stand aside from my
body. I was not falling, for the reason that I was not in a
dimension where it was possible to fall. I, that is my consciousness, was apart from my body, and not in the least
concerned with what was befalling it. My body was in the
process of being injured, crushed and pulped, and my consciousness was not associated with these physical injuries, and
was completely uninterested in them.[3]

3

The second mode of access by living persons to further worlds
is one which requires a training in extension of consciousness
to which Rudolf Steiner gives the name of 'Spiritual Science'.
This awakens interior faculties of vision. The important difference between this and the passive telepathic process is that the
spiritual scientist claims that he can then bring to bear his own
powers of observation and judgement, instead of having to rely
upon the accounts of others. If many more people succeed in
training themselves as spiritual scientists and can bring about
observations which are broadly in accord with one another,
then the evidence would become more solid and difficult to
dispute. Rudolf Steiner, who held a Viennese doctorate in
philosophy, possessed extra-sensory faculties from his childhood.
His pupils find that the faculty requires strict discipline and is
hard to acquire.

This material also has a severe methodological limitation for,
though we now have a witness we can examine and who is free
to proceed with his own direct observations, most of us in turn
have to rely upon his description, just as we have to rely
similarly upon a telepathic communicator.

Steiner's picture of the spiritual worlds on the whole tallies
well with what the deeper discarnate stories tell us. Part of his
vision looks a long way beyond early discarnate experiences. Few
could seriously study discarnate accounts without acquiring a
deep respect for Rudolf Steiner. But observation with the aid of

spiritual science, as by any other process, cannot guarantee to overcome the personal perceptual limitations of whoever practises it. Steiner, who disliked adulation, warned his followers that some of his own observations would certainly turn out to be incorrect.

So we are once again confronted with a hearsay factor. All these sources alike can be judged only as reports on the experiences – truly or falsely recounted – of other persons.

The Peak in Darien reports – and this is important – have a further severe limitation. They describe only what can be observed from the threshold; they are glimpses into a next world, they are not journeys into the interior. Indeed these narrators often reach a point when they are shown that further access to a world beyond is at present to be denied them.

Such experiences are curtain raisers. They may be truly anticipatory. But by definition they cannot include any transforming experiences, which come about only as a result of death itself.

Of these three sources of information, the most widely based is that which claims to be direct discarnate telepathic communication.

4

It is of course essential to assess the intentions of a communicator for good or evil. This is a prime factor in judgement. When the possibility of visitors from outer space is discussed, our first reaction is often that they must be hostile. As a result of religious fears, discarnate beings are frequently regarded in the same way. Fear of communication with the dead lies deep within the fold of orthodoxy. Honest pastoral care often forbids attempts to look beyond the veil.

This prohibition springs from this fear that information from communicators could be gravely misleading, or must come from evil sources. Many earnest and devout Christians believe that the Bible prohibits communication. But this is in no way the clear-cut issue pastoral care usually preaches. As words and

concepts change down the centuries, biblical texts lose some of
the shades of meanings they conveyed to former translators.
They are seen to reflect the climate of their time and need to be
reinterpreted nearer to the original texts. For instance, as theological scholars like the Revd D. J. Bretherton and the Revd L.
Argyll have recently shown, necromancy in biblical times was
very properly condemned, but not as communication *per se*. It
was because it made use of black magical practices:

> As such they are an abomination of the Lord Yahweh and an
> offence to His holy Name. They represent primitive orgiastic
> attempts through false deities and magic formulae and the
> use of dead bodies to obtain information normally hidden
> from human understanding. All this stands in vivid contrast
> to the recognised seers and prophets of Israel whose psychical
> and spiritual gifts of sensitivity and insight were dedicated to
> the work and service of Yahweh, the God of Israel.[4]

In naming the woman of Endor a witch, the King James
translators reflected the persecutory spirit of their own and
earlier times:

> The dread of witchcraft and its horrific associations has influ-
> enced the translation of the Deuteronomic formula in the
> Geneva Bible which in turn influenced subsequent versions,
> including the Bishop's Bible, the Authorised Version of King
> James, the Revised Version and modern renderings.[5]

The translation speaks of calling up spirits but, as anyone
today can readily discover for themselves, it is not possible to
call up the spirit of a particular person at will. Indeed an indirect
factor for the authenticity of communication is that the communicator most desired often does not appear, though others
may do so instead. Those who point to the Witch of Endor story
as condemning all communication as evil surely ought then to
ask why Samuel consented to take part in it.

Communications are frequent in the lives of saints, whether
regarded as angelic visitations or as vivid telepathic impressions.

The saints have shown their stature by an incomparable power of utilising such impressions for the deepening of their spiritual insights.

> All these great and generous souls persist in ever using these psycho-physical things, whether they be projections or 'givennesses', as but so many instruments and materials for the apprehension, illustration, acquisition, and purification of spiritual truth and of the spirit's own fulness and depth.[6]

> Indeed all the great mystics, and this in precise proportion to their greatness, have ever taught that . . . visions and voices are to be accepted by the mind only in proportion as they convey some spiritual truth of importance to it or to others, and as they actually help it to become more humble, true, and loving.[7]

Thus these impressions have sometimes formed a prime source for interior spiritual riches.

Canons for distinguishing healthy from unhealthy paranormal experiences of this kind in the lives of the saints are fully and carefully analysed in Baron von Hugel's *The Mystical Element of Religion*.[8]

The Psychic Life of Jesus, by the Revd Maurice Elliott, shows that Jesus too made use of His extra-sensory perceptions. Because of this, some Spiritualistic opinion turns Him into no more than a super-medium, but of course extra-sensory faculties are only a part of His spiritual equipment, as they were in the saints. Nevertheless, He did not scruple to use them.

To some the most important statement of all which Jesus has made concerning survival of death is implicit in the very fact of His appearances to His disciples after the Crucifixion.

The essential Easter good news is that He lived on. He was willing moreover to appear many times to His disciples to show that He did. Moses and Elias appeared at the Transfiguration. So both before and after His death He participated in spiritual psychic communications. Those who accept His divinity sometimes say that Jesus Christ is in a special situation. Surely, then, all the more would Jesus as our exemplar not break the spiritual law in order to make these appearances. By sanctioning the principle of communication, however, He very obviously did not sanction it at a low level and for evil purposes. Hence the need for Paul's later tests of the fruits of the spirit. These are weighty theological matters, but any clear-sighted Bible reader today surely needs to come to terms with those events and teachings in the New Testament which cast a critical light on any statement that communication with the dead is always evil.

The situation has been excellently weighed up recently by Chancellor the Revd E. Garth Moore :

> It is clearly impossible to extract from the Bible a condem-nation of everything psychic . . . for it would involve the con-demnation of an innate quality which, whether they enjoy it or not, some persons possess and which perhaps is latent in all persons. Any such condemnation would include our Lord himself within its ambit, for he exhibited ESP in a marked degree. The attack presumably is confined to certain psychic practices. But, even when the attack is thus limited, it is difficult to sustain . . .
>
> But that is not to suggest that the Bible is to be ignored. One thing emerges clearly from an over-all reading of it, namely, that our God-given talents, whatever they be, should be used to the glory of the God who has given them. To pervert them to other purposes may well be to fall within the Levitical condemnations. A good discretion is required, and wariness is to be commended.[9]

5

There are two other ways in which theological reasoning and speculation today are operating against any direct examination of the evidence. The first is the demythologising school of thought, which, along with other influences, is producing some students in theological college who do not even accept a doctrine of sur-vival of death. The second is the doctrine of eternal life as a quality of consciousness, to attain to which is the soul's true destiny, with the practical rider that this eternal life so far exceeds in quality any mere survival of the soul and personality after death that no consideration need be paid to the latter. The implication is that the greater surpasses the lesser. So indeed it may, but does not the recipient need to work to be worthy of it, and cast off those parts of himself which do not bear the qualities of eternal life? Is it not more reasonable that there is an interim period of purgatory (which many accounts describe) when sinners can repent, and good folk can learn how gradually to cast off limitations of being which make it impossible for them as yet to sustain eternal life? A doctrine of purgatory implies a personal survival of death and an intermediary period of learning. Very many Christians will find no need to quarrel with that.

6

It is very sad that, because of the lack of a spirit of exploration, many clergy in the Anglican faith in speaking about survival and its parallel, the communion of saints, are able to give little comfort to the newly bereaved, who are left feeling that life has become pointless and empty. Such clergymen remain reluctant (and are sometimes under pressure to remain so) to examine for themselves the direct evidence at first hand or in books. Their prior condemnation of it prevents them from doing so.

On the other hand, the standard view presented in Spiritualist churches does not often look much further than to an idealised, quasi-material replica of life on earth, a gratifying land to which all are admitted after a decent interval. Such pseudo-realistic accounts, when repeated often enough, receive popular and uncritical acceptance amongst those who find it easy to take as literal what is often intended to be approximate or metaphorical, and who are altogether too easily satisfied.

Hundreds of communications whilst not of any profundity are loving and helpful, and of transparent good will. It is also perfectly true that not all communications are of this kind. We are on realistic ground in declaring that communications can be either good or evil. How then can we distinguish the latter? Evil-doers are skilled in exploiting character weaknesses in the recipient. They flatter, threaten, and try to obtain power over him. Communications which do not seek to gain any power over the reader are likely to be of good intent. Those primarily concerned with describing the afterlife consistently paint the power of good there and the folly of evil. It is therefore unreasonable to condemn discarnate communications as a whole.

If anyone's Christian scruples have hitherto held him back, let him by all means preserve his scruples but ask whether what he finds in the more specifically Christian part of the accounts justifies those scruples or causes them to melt gradually away. The best answer to feeling afraid of these accounts is to look at them with all due care and then let the heart and mind accept such part, if any, as they tell him to accept. Many Christians, including a number of ordained ministers, have already taken such a course and later found themselves ready to extend their psychic studies.

The Revd Harold Anson, former Master of the Temple, a fair-minded first-hand student and one who rightly remained very critical of much in Spiritualism, writes:

> It is often asserted that Spiritualism leads men away from Christianity. This may, in many cases, well be true, especially when Christianity has only been known in one of its more debased forms. But I have known many whose Christian faith has been notably confirmed and deepened by psychical experience.
>
> The experience of the Revd A. Webling in *Something Beyond* where he relates how he had almost abandoned all belief in God, and was afterwards brought back to a full belief in the Christian gospel by psychic experience, is by no means peculiar. I know very many men and women who have been confirmed and established in their faith through Spiritualism.
>
> The danger which Spiritualism no doubt offers is mainly to those whose hold upon the unseen world is either

undeveloped or non-existent. Where the Christian Faith offers a realized and tangible link with the unseen world, and people are able to say, 'I know that the spiritual world exists and that the Communion of Saints is a reality', the baser forms of 'Spiritualism' will offer no attraction.[10]

He might also have added, which would be true, that through discarnate communication many others, neither Christians nor Spiritualists, have gained on effective realisation of the spiritual world.

Here are the Revd Webling's own words:

Psychical research is attracting the attention of an increasing number of thoughtful people in all grades of life, who realize that, unless a considerable body of persons otherwise notable for their intellectual pre-eminence have taken leave of their senses, conclusions of an importance not easily measured have already been reached about man's nature, powers and destiny. For, to my mind, the evidence is conclusive of much more than survival. It is, of course, obvious that reports on the nature of life beyond the grave cannot normally be tested in the same way as we can the evidence for survival itself. But if it be granted that communication with the departed exists, and the truthfulness of messages thus obtained is established in matters capable of verification, then it is, at least, not improbable that information gathered from the same sources, even if at present unverifiable, may yet be true. And when the information given at various times through half a century, and in all parts of the world, is in substantial agreement, and is, moreover, though often of a kind unexpected by a particular recipient, yet inherently probable and consistent with that given to others, then, as it seems to me, the cumulative effect is weighty.[11]

7

We must inquire into the integrity of those who receive these telepathic communications. How do they approach their work?

The more serious-minded the sensitive, the more frequently he or she is likely to feel periods of doubt. Most find it hard to come to terms with their material. Fear of self-delusion is almost a signature tune in the make-up of serious sensitives. None escapes it altogether.

Where the sensitive is a priest, misgivings as to the moral intentions of the communicator are especially likely to arise in addition to the normal fear of sensitives that the material springs entirely from their own mind.

There is an opinion abroad that the clergy are very credulous beings. But our training in the exercise of the critical faculty places us among the most hard-to-convince when any new truth is in question. It took a quarter of a century to convince me – ten years that spirit communication was a fact, and fifteen that the fact was legitimate and good.

. . . I received requests that I would sit quietly, pencil in hand, and take down any thoughts which seemed to come into my mind projected there by some external personality and not consequent on the exercise of my own mentality. Reluctance lasted a long time, but at last I felt that friends were at hand who wished very earnestly to speak with me. They did not overrule or compel my will in any way – that would have settled the matter at once, so far as I was concerned – but their wishes were made ever more plain.

I felt at last that I ought to give them an opportunity, for I was impressed with the feeling that the influence was a good one, and so, at last, very doubtfully, I decided to sit in my cassock in the vestry after Evensong.[12]

That is how the Revd Vale Owen came to terms with his own conscience. Vale Owen particularly impressed Lord Northcliffe, because when the scripts came to be published he refused to take any money for them.

Amongst the large number of scripts received by the Revd Stainton Moses, another Anglican parson and an English master for eighteen years at University College School, many represent a long intellectual struggle through which his former theological view eventually became modified and broadened. These scripts are of special interest as we can watch the communicator week by week dealing firmly, fairly and very earnestly with the clergyman's difficulties and resistances. Stainton Moses thus describes the tests and standards he applied to his own scripts:

> It is an interesting subject for speculation whether my own thoughts entered into the subject-matter of the communications. I took extraordinary pains to prevent any such admixture. . . . Very soon the messages assumed a character of which I had no doubt whatever that the thought was opposed to my own. But I cultivated the power of occupying my mind with other things during the time that the writing was going on, and was able to read an abstruse book, and follow out a line of close reasoning, while the message was written with unbroken regularity . . .
>
> I am not, however, concerned to contend that my own mind was not utilised, or that what was thus written did not depend for its form on the mental qualifications of the medium through whom it was given. So far as I know, it is always the case. . . . It is not conceivable that it should be otherwise. But it is certain that the mass of ideas conveyed to me were alien to my own opinion, were in the main opposed to my settled convictions. . . .
>
> I never could command the writing. It came unsought usually: and when I did seek it, as often as not I was unable of obtain it. A sudden impulse, coming I knew not how, led me to sit down and prepare to write. Where the messages were in regular course, I was accustomed to devote the first hour of each day to sitting for their reception. I rose early, and the beginning of the day was spent, in a room that I used for no other purpose, in what was to all intents and purposes a religious service. . . .
>
> The particular communications, which I received from the spirit known to me as Imperator, mark a distinct epoch in my life. I have noted . . . the intense exaltation of spirit, the strenuous conflict, the intervals of peace that I have since longed for, but have seldom attained, which marked their transmission. It was a period of education in which I underwent a spiritual development that was, in its outcome, a very

regeneration. . . . It may possibly be borne in upon the minds of some, who are not ignorant of the dispensation of the Spirit in their own inner selves, that for me the question of the beneficent action of external Spirit on my own self was then finally settled. I have never since, even in the vagaries of an extremely sceptical mind, and amid much cause for questioning, ever seriously entertained a doubt.[13]

Rather different difficulties arose for Geraldine Cummins, perhaps the best and most versatile of all scriptwriters. Her work ranges from the Cleophas historical narratives which impressed a number of Christian scholars and theologians, to scripts from the naturalist Eric Parker, and to F. W. H. Myers's description of the afterlife. 'Directed writing' is the term she prefers for her work. A difficulty which sometimes faced her lay in being asked when strangers were present to launch herself into the somewhat rarefied area of awareness where she felt she could obtain material not originated by herself and which did not come from another mind on earth. On a few occasions she did find herself tuning in to a mind on earth, as when with W. B. Yeats present she produced a script which he said exactly mirrored his own ideas in a play he was then writing about Jonathan Swift. Geraldine Cummins gives a very clear description of what her working method entailed. (The poet A. E. in his lifetime helped her to develop it.)

In order to enter the stillness, it is necessary to raise one's intelligence to a higher degree of consciousness. The stillness is neither a passive, inert state, nor trance, in my experience. When achieved it is a lucid work of intense activity. The condition of stillness clarifies the desire and creates efficiency. . . .
. . . This procedure, if successfully practised, releases me from the material world. A condition of complete inattention to life is my goal, then a 'not-self' seems to dictate. . . .
. . . I am as a stenographer taking down words from dictation and employing as it were an inner hearing. . . Of course, I have had my blank sittings devoid of evidence.[14]

Mrs Willett, who after her death produced scripts via Geraldine Cummins and who at times treated her distinctly haughtily as her amanuensis, nevertheless sympathised with the characteristic lack of confidence which sensitives feel. She says :

> When we converse . . . with a medium or automatist we become, as it were, dependent on her thoughts, words and images, and we go wrong, we stray in that tide. It can be a River of Forgetfulness temporarily too, for the struggling communicator in many cases, and it can be a mixture; part the automatist, part the communicator, or it can come in flashes and be almost true. I say this for your encouragement, as I see how much you doubt and want to be done with it all. I know those moods. I had them at times.[15]

The writer of *The Betty Book* had to undertake a somewhat parallel course to that of Geraldine Cummins in learning to transfer consciousness to another layer of her mind. It required a considerable struggle before she mastered it. These very interesting scripts show the large part the communicators themselves played in urging and disciplining this writer to reach and hold the consciousness necessary. They show too how hard it was for her to retain it once she had reached it, a phenomenon which Mrs Willett also knew well; she frequently complained of its difficulty.

> . . . she slipped . . . into a kind of freed or double consciousness. From it she reported various experiences. Her speech was at first halting and stumbling, her phrases fragmentary, as though she were having great difficulty. Apparently this was due to the necessity for running two consciousnesses at once. The normal, from which she spoke, was subordinate, it seemed; her real awareness being centred in a deeper consciousness, from which she reported back. . . .
> The idea seemed to be that Betty was to be brought in touch, through the superconsciousness, with realities which she absorbed direct, and with ideas conveyed sometimes in words heard with the 'inner ear', sometimes by mental impression. These things she transferred down to her habitual con-

sciousness, which then reported them to me.

She constantly complained of the dilution caused by this transfer. What reached the paper was, according to her, but an unsatisfactory pale shadow of the actuality.[16]

Here is another requirement.

What we want is not merely facility, but a trained intelligent co-operation . . . Only thus can we command . . . reliability. . . .

Attested phenomena of a spontaneous . . . character are produced, or made possible at all, by a condition of extreme flexibility . . . Plasticity and pliability are essential, splicing both the higher and lower consciousnesses. Rigidity permits no impress.[17]

8

How much are even serious script-writers likely to contribute out of themselves to these scripts? This obviously varies greatly, both between one writer and another, and also between a writer at her best and the same writer at something near her worst.

Geraldine Cummins, for instance, started a number of scripts which rapidly petered out; one claimed to be, but clearly was not, from Sappho. Her inner discipline enabled her in time to distinguish scripts which had no supporting substance from the claimed communicator. Compared with Geraldine, Vale Owen's possible compass was obviously very much narrower; his mind was set firmly into ecclesiastical concepts. His scripts about post-mortem life contain numerous accounts of church ceremonies. Being a cleric surely influenced where his mind could take him; his communicators, unlike some of Geraldine's, shared his interests and concerns. His normal equipment was both a strength and a limitation. This must always be the case with the script-writer. Mrs Willett's aesthetic sense sharpened the area where her communicators could work with her help. They could appeal to her sense of beauty and to her keen sensibility as a woman; this was a great asset.

Without Stainton Moses's theological training, his scripts too could not have taken the form they did. His theological problems of conscience formed his best area of attention and contributed to the scripts, as Mrs Willett's poetic sensibility did to hers. The communicators aim to make use of the recipient's qualities to help them to say what they wish (and sometimes, no doubt, these same qualities also limit them). They are the architects and the recipient provides the building materials.

The distinction between communicator and recipient can never be made with perfect sharpness. The purposes of the two concerned and the talents each have available blend, but can also become confused and out of resonance with one another. At times it can be anything but a smooth collaboration. To the communicator it must sometimes seem like attempting to steer an obstinate and high-mettled horse without a bridle down a traffic-busy and noisy road,. with many obstructing vehicles representing the jostling contents of the recipient's own mind.

The relative contribution of communicator and recipient can also vary from script to script and from moment to moment in the same script. The communicator of course plays the dominant role, the task of the recipient being to reflect the author's meaning much as a pianist interprets the composer as faithfully as he can.

The better equipped the recipient, the richer the partnership can be, provided the dominant and subservient roles are preserved. But this is not easily attained, for passivity and flexibility are the essential qualities needed, and some communicators seemingly prefer to settle for these, rather than for a trained but intellect-bound mind. Yet, without a recipient of trained mind, we would never, for instance, have received the interesting series of scripts which Lawrence Hyde – himself a professional author and philosopher – wrote rapidly at the rate of a chapter a day from what he believed to be the dictation of a group of discarnate philosophers headed by George Santayana. His trained intellectual acuity enabled him to apprehend the sort of distinctions his communicators wished to impart. Here we see the collaborative side of partnership at its most distinctive.

Because he provided building materials of the quality needed, we can of course reach the point of accusing Lawrence Hyde of being his own architect as well. This risk is run by all script-writers of intellectual calibre. Lawrence Hyde certainly did not think the material was his : he said the 'feel' of the process was quite different from when he was writing from himself.

> In the phenomenal universe the permanent and the imper-manent are indissolubly conjoined. And they are also sub-jectively conjoined within the individual when wisdom and love have become united in his being. It will thus be seen that a triple synthesis is entailed : within the subject, within man's being, and between man's being and the external world.
>
> This condition is actually experienced by the illuminate. The effect is that he overcomes the distinction between himself and that which is outside himself, realising that the self and the notself represent the two complementary poles of one fundamental state of being. As a consequence the realm of phenomena becomes invested for him with an eternal character, while at the same time his interior being is enlarged and consolidated through his having in a metaphysical sense absorbed the outer world into himself.
>
> He finds also that the relations presented to him in the external world become fully intelligible only when everything is considered in relation to that whole in which all things are comprehended. He further perceives that he cannot separate himself fundamentally from any other living being, and that he is one in essence with the Creator of the universe. Finally, he attains to the sublime realisation that in their interior aspect all things are One.[18]

Script-writers often claim that the great speed at which they work, far faster than a writer's normal capability, is evidence of their discarnate source. I find this an unconvincing argument. It shows no more than that they work in a state of partial dissociation. The quality of the text is a far better criterion than the mode of production. Seriousness of purpose, watchfulness, wariness, self-discipline and strenuous effort to reach and maintain the right level of consciousness are the hallmarks of the best script writers.

In the next chapter we will examine how some travellers describe the way in which they have passed through the barrier of death and tell us that they find their identity to be still intact.

PART TWO

The Narratives

CHAPTER 5

Early Experiences

1

The two ideas inevitably linked with death are extinction and judgement, and these convey mutually conflicting concepts of finality. However, when travellers' tales claiming to describe life after death are examined, nothing of finality emerges at all.

The traveller's own view is at first a very incomplete one. He is only in an ante-room. His experience is unplumbed. Early accounts will not and cannot be wholly realistic. If humans carry over something of their old selves, they are highly likely to carry over something of their former personal limitations as well. The idea of gaining any final knowledge about life by the simple act of dying is absurd, and found nowhere in these travellers' tales. To expect that death will reveal all, like a card player throwing his hand down on the table, is about as true as that marriage brings happiness ever afterwards. We learn, the travellers say, a little by dying, but much more by continuing to live on. Immediately after death, as F. W. H. Myers has declared, the new arrival knows little more of the true nature of his environment than a babe does of earth life. The difference, of course, is that he is able to bring to it an adult consciousness.

It is natural to suppose that all men must meet the same experience in death. Yet on earth we know that the physical incident of death and the inner psychological events preceding it are not the same for all. Death and its accompanying events treat people differently, as life on earth treats them differently. In the same way after-death experiences are not always the same, nor encountered in the same order. There appear to be considerable differences, dependent upon the make-up of the individual. We shall see that some people adapt themselves swiftly; some resist their environment and shut themselves into a mental prison, alone or with others; others withdraw and wait and rest. Many are chiefly concerned with finding those persons with whom their earth life was intermeshed. A person's temperament, if only for the time being, remains much the same as on earth.

2

The first surprise in the reports is the insistence upon the painlessness of the actual process of dying. Indeed, a large majority of those communicators who trouble to describe it (and many do not) declare that the actual incident of death, whatever pain may have preceded it, was in itself almost completely painless. The report is often that the death was not recognised until it was over, and sometimes not even then. Those unprepared for death, or those who encounter sudden death, frequently fail to understand what has happened. Even when expected there is often surprise that so little seems to have happened. There is sometimes, for instance, little sense of any 'journey'.

No one will deny the severity and reality of pain in many terminal illnesses, but the death agony and the transition itself frequently appear to be accompanied and preceded by a dissociation of consciousness which includes freedom from most, or sometimes all, of the physical pain. The participant, looking back on it, paints a much more favourable picture than an onlooker.

Here are some posthumous comments:

They do not suffer, these people, in their passing. I think sometimes their friends suffer more, when they see the bodies writhing in apparent agony, while in reality the spirit is already tasting the first freedom from pain, or lies in a blessed insensibility.[1]

From F. W. H. Myers:

> Death is . . . a mere episode which we regard with a certain
> tenderness and not with any pain . . . there is contained in it
> a time of stillness, of sinking gloriously into rest.[2]

Sir Alvary Gascoigne, a diplomat, tells of his own death to his
sister, Cynthia, Lady Sandys:

> Every part of me seemed to be switching off gently, and . . .
> I suddenly found I was floating above my body . . . Nothing
> in life comes up to the immense joy of dying . . . I told you
> that I had experienced a strange feeling of power that seemed
> to be drawing me out of my body during the last few days of
> my illness. . . . I welcomed this inrush of new life and let go
> very willingly. That was why I did not linger . . . You must
> . . . be ready to receive the power that draws you quite pain-
> lessly out of your body. It's the most beautiful and glorious
> thing. I see so many are prolonging their life quite unneces-
> sarily. . . . Life commands; you agree and co-operate.[3]

Wellesley Tudor Pole describes his own psychic perception of the
workings of the death process in his friend, Major P., and the
Major's own comments subsequently. Wellesley Tudor Pole was
well aware of the evidential limitations inherent in his account.

First, his observations of his friend's dying: the notes were
made within a few hours of actual events.

> 22nd March, 3 p.m. Death seems very close at hand . . .
> Directly above the dying man I can see a shadowy form that
> hovers in a horizontal position about two feet above the bed.
> This form is attached to the physical body . . . by two trans-
> parent elastic cords. One of them appears to be attached to
> the solar plexus and the other to the brain. As I watch this
> form it grows more distinct in outline, until I can see that it
> is an exact counterpart. . . . I can see what look like spiral
> currents passing up through these two cords, and as the
> physical body grows more lifeless, the form hovering above
> seems to become vital.

3.15 p.m. Two figures have now appeared, and stand one on either side of the bed . . . These forms seem . . . to be of some finer form of 'matter' than the 'double' that is hovering above the bed.

3.40 p.m. This 'double' has become still more distinct . . . The life-force is steadily ebbing out of the body, and is apparently passing into the form above.

3.55 p.m. The two figures stoop down over the bed and seem to break off the 'cords' at points close to the physical body. Immediately . . . the form or double rises about two feet from its original position, but remains horizontal, and at this same moment Major P.'s heart stops beating. . . .

4.30 p.m. The dead man seems to be asleep within . . . [his] new garment, and is totally dissociated from the body on the bed.

Now for the event, as subsequently recorded by Major P. himself :

An overpowering feeling that I am about to sever my connection with earth-life comes over me. Yet I am still myself, and still, physically speaking, in bed . . .

Now I see . . . myself; but can that be myself? That form lying there asleep among the trees . . . in that fair land . . .

Why, it is as if I were in pieces! No, not that, but rather as if I were extracting the real 'me' from the unreal 'me'; . . . I am *still*! Thank God for that! To rest and listen, and no longer to be afraid, to feel *safe*; it is wonderful.[4]

Helen Salter, the psychical researcher and one of the automatists of the cross-correspondence tests, describes her death thus to her husband :

. . . my turn to make what some believe is a long journey. But for me it was such a short journey. Oh, it was so incredibly easy and painless. There was only one very brief nightmare, when I wanted to get back into my body in order to return to you. An instant's bad dream. That's all death was to me. After it, almost immediately, there came the unimaginable moment – a welcoming mother and father. You can't imagine what a feeling of safety they gave me. Freedom at once from that inert thing, my body – freedom from the fear of the Unknown . . .

In the past we, you and I, have wondered what our arrival to this level would be like. But nothing we supposed came up to that beautiful, surprising, homely feeling I had with these two protectors waiting for me. That's why I have called it the unimaginable moment.

Death's exit is so simple, and all our lives we have made it intrinsically complicated . . .[5]

3

Where consciousness remains intact before impending death some report visions of dead friends and, as a result of it, find themselves reconciled to their coming death and looking forward to it. These experiences become hard to explain away as non-veridical hallucinations when the dying recipients appear to remain in every other way rational, and when what they see affects them with as much or more emotional impact than many normal experiences. These experiences can be perfectly distinct.

Horace Traubel was a poet of Walt Whitman's school. Mrs Flora Macdonald-Denison, who was present at Traubel's death-bed, recounts:

. . . All day on August 28th Horace [had been] very low-spirited. He had been brought in from the veranda but was now absolutely radiant. 'Look, look, Flora, quick, quick, he is going!' 'What, where, Horace, I do not see anyone.' 'Why, just over the rock Walt appeared, head and shoulders and hat on in a golden glory; brilliant and splendid. He reassured me, beckoned to me, and spoke to me. I heard his voice but did not understand all he said: only "Come on" '. All the rest of the evening Horace was uplifted and happy. . . .

On the night of September 3rd Horace was very low. Then he said: 'I hear Walt's voice, he is talking to me'. I said: 'What does he say?' He said: 'Walt says: "Come on, come on" '. After a time he said : 'Flora, I see them all about me, Bob and Bucke and Walt, and the rest . . .'[6]

Colonel Cosgrave, also present at Traubel's deathbed, had his own confirming experience :

> On the last night, about 3 a.m., he grew perceptibly weaker, and his eyes opened, staring towards the further side of the bed, his lips moved, endeavouring to speak; his eyes remained riveted on a point some three feet above the bed. My eyes were at last drawn irresistibly to the same point in the darkness. Slowly the point at which we were both looking grew gradually brighter, a light haze appeared, spreading until it assumed bodily form, and took the likeness of Walt Whitman, standing upright beside the bed, a rough tweed jacket on, an old felt hat upon his head, and his right hand in his pocket, similar to a number of his portraits, he was gazing down at Traubel, a kindly reassuring smile upon his face, he nodded twice as though reassuringly, the features quite distinct for at least a full minute, then gradually faded from sight.[7]

A likeness wearing old clothes will provoke scepticism in some; more will be said about this later. Since the image resembled known portraits, the Colonel may too have contributed something of himself to what he saw.

Do such visions also occur sometimes when the dying person does not report them or is unable to do so? Similar experiences to these received before death are certainly supplemented and supported in some retrospective accounts of the aftermath, the recognition that death has taken place, and the return to consciousness.

> I remember feeling rather peculiar, I suppose it would be the night before I passed over. I did not think I was going, but felt less clear in mind than usual. About dawn I had a sinking feeling, and the daylight seemed to go. I seemed to be swaying about in the dark and felt slightly giddy. Then the atmosphere seemed to become light around me and I heard

voices, but they were not the voices of the people on earth, they were the voices of my two dear boys, the voices I had not heard for many long years. I did not feel impatient, I knew they were there and that I should not lose them again. I was content to wait until I should be able to speak to them. I did not feel that wild joy, that great elation, that I had always expected to feel. I was not in the state for it, but felt heavy, stupid and sleepy, yet at peace and full of confidence and quiet happiness knowing they were round me. Now and again I heard other voices, but they seemed far away. I suppose those were the voices of people actually in the room with me. The nearer voices were those of my boys.

After a time of unconsciousness I seemed to have become clearer quite suddenly. It was like a burst of sunshine, and I looked. I seemed able to move my eyes quite suddenly, and in the burst of sight and light I saw my boys, my brothers, and many others round me. I think this was only for a moment or two and then I must have gone to sleep again. I knew nothing more then, and so suppose that it was just before leaving my body that I had that burst of light. I remember waking gradually on this side and hearing one of my sons say : 'Be quiet and don't try to think'.[8]

4

In order to understand the varying nature of the experiences met with soon after death, it is essential to grasp that the event is not nearly so important, in the scale of discarnate values, as we usually expect. Differences in individual experience of death then become both less significant and less apparently unjust than they can seem at first sight. The differences which arise in passing through the incident of death fall into four main categories :

1 Some find it is incomprehensible that it has happened and for some considerable time persist in believing themselves to be still on earth, and hence suffer a state of confusion.

I am still rather puzzled as regards the actual events before my decease. I just remember the great darkness swooping down on me like a bird. How close, how suffocating it was. Then at last, there was relief, expansion, a sense of being freed from an intolerable weight. When I came out into a strange clearness, I did not believe that I had died. . . . My memory isn't quite the same, at least so far. It is as if a curtain had been rung on a play. I know it has all happened, is, perhaps, still there in its setting behind that curtain. But I can't quite visualise it. I suppose I am not much older as regards time. There is no Big Ben here.[9]

2 Others, particularly those who have long been ill, drift in and out of consciousness; their readjustment is gradual, and punctuated by sleep. The new arrival has to overcome gradually the weariness which was in the mind and feelings during the last days, and which sometimes remains. Periods of unconsciousness are part of a pattern of adjustment, enabling a more gradual and easy facing of the new experiences bit by bit between each such period of rest.

The spirit longs to rest, there comes the great desire to sleep.

In that sleep a great deal happens but I don't know enough yet to tell you all about it. It is not exactly a sleep, but your sleep in the earth life is very much the nearest thing to it . . . All you know is that you wake up another being. When the spirit comes out of that sleep he knows where he is and what he is, as you sometimes wake up in the morning with some knotty problem solved.

Those who pass over with full knowledge and understanding of the life beyond do not need that sleep at all, unless they come over with their spirits tired by long illness or the worries of life. In practice almost everyone needs the sleep period for a shorter or a longer time. The greater the difficulty of the spirit in adjusting himself to the new conditions, the longer and deeper the sleep period that is necessary.

How to describe what it feels like when you come out of that sleep. You know quite clearly that you are alive, without any muddle about thinking that you are still in the earth life. During that experience something has taught us and told us.[10]

This script from her brother was received by Zöe Richmond, another member of the cross-correspondence group.

Frances Banks, the former nun, became perfectly aware of her impending death; almost her last words were: 'The change has started.' She talks of her first impression after death:

> After the Change was over and I was free of my earthly 'covering' I 'woke up' here . . . I opened my eyes . . . or I came back to consciousness . . . and there was Mother Superior just as she used to be and as I had remembered her for so many years.
>   She took my hand. She said 'So you have arrived safely?'[11]

Then she sank into unconsciousness again, to awake from time to time to find herself gazing at another old friend, now re-met; later becoming aware, by a telepathic pull, of her friends at her cremation; and again, finding herself looking in at the memorial service being held for her in Exeter Cathedral. Only after a further period of unconsciousness did her active discarnate life begin.

Yet, meanwhile, this telepathic pull from her friends on earth, as they thought about her with unusual intensity, was effective in reaching and awakening her mind. Telepathic rapport is common in the early days after death, and can initiate itself either from those on earth or from the one on the other side of death; the links of feeling and thought remain, and for a brief while seem particularly easy to activate. The one who has died is at first accessible in this immediately realisable way. Later it will require a closer tie of affinity or the sharing of a common task, and may lessen or cease through the competing pull of other tasks in the world beyond death.

3 Many die without preconception of what, if anything, they will encounter. The mental furniture they carried about on earth, which some still cling on to, delays the processes of adjustment.

You must not think that directly he awakes to his next state of being a man recognises that old springs of action are no longer effective. He still imagines that he must satisfy his hunger and seek wealth, love or ease in one accustomed way or another. He does not at once perceive that, though so many of his surroundings are unexpectedly familiar, actually conditions have enormously changed. Then come instructors, and his friends, if he has any, intervene and try to explain things to him. But it is extraordinary how deaf a large number of persons remain to this information. In many cases they believe that they are being deceived, or are dreaming in a new way. This latter view is that most commonly held; nothing will persuade them they are dead. It is not their idea of death, neither the heaven nor the hell that a common religious teaching leads them to expect, and they hold out stubbornly in their belief.[12]

4 Those who die by accident or violence find it less easy, according to some writers, to adjust than do those who die naturally, although this may not always be the case.

Those who are killed quite suddenly . . . come over with the feelings and thoughts which they had just before, often it is those who still think they have to go on fighting and have to be calmed; often they think they must have suddenly gone mad, because the scene has changed. That is not surprising if you can imagine in what a tremendous state of tension, almost like madness, the actual fighting is carried out. Then they often think . . . they are now in a base hospital. . . .

We have to humour them at first and only gradually explain to them what the hospital means. Sometimes they are profoundly glad, those who have come to the limit of endurance, and rejoice to be free from the world of wars. Sometimes, with those who have very strong home ties, we have to let them realise as gently and gradually as possible; most are so weary in spirit that they worry very little, and are soon ready to settle down to their rest.

Others have foreseen that they must be killed, they have seen the shell or bomb about to explode, and have known that when it explodes they must go.[13]

Many describe an awakening in an unknown beautiful landscape, or in a hospital. This is sometimes puzzling to them. These are best regarded as interim experiences, a preliminary emotional therapy before deeper rehabilitation comes about.

5

Those who have expected to survive death, and already knew something about communication with the dead, usually find it easier to make the adjustment.

From where she found herself reclining she looked through an open doorway into a garden of flowers, and realised that she was in the home which had been described by her father in his communications. While gazing out upon the scene of beauty and light she became aware that her father was standing near. They did not immediately speak in words, but it seemed to her that they were *thinking to each other*, exchanging ideas mentally without spoken words. When, presently, he spoke she found it delightful to hear his voice again, and to be able to reply in the old, familiar way.[14]

Some months later she said :

It is difficult to realise I have been here so long a time, it seems no more than a few weeks; for there is so much to do, to see, and to learn. I am glad to have known before my passing something about this life and the possibilities of communication with you. Before finally leaving earth I seemed to be dreaming, and yet it was not wholly a dream. It seemed as if I had come here before the final separation from my physical body. I was only partly conscious towards the last, only half within the body; for my soul was already freeing itself. Nor did it seem wholly strange to me when I found myself here. I must have frequently come during sleep; for I could now remember that I had been here previously.[15]

It is natural enough that some of those who have not expected to survive, or who have long abandoned any judgement on the matter, find it harder to understand their new situation, and they may be for a while unable or reluctant to do so.

Some, in the early stages, even endeavour to continue to take part in events on earth. This indeed is one of the most common, if painful, ways in which the survivor eventually becomes persuaded that he has died, and yet still exists.

Some recognise their condition by glimpsing their own relatives on earth, and finding them mourning. They may speak to them and then become bewildered and afraid because they do not receive any answer, or even any recognition that they are present. They begin to wonder if they are mad, dreaming, or at least ill and mentally confused. Edgar Wallace described what seemed to him a papier mâché effigy of himself, lying in a coffin. Extremely angry at what he thought a joke in very bad taste, nevertheless (he says) somewhere deep within him there arose what at that moment seemed a dread truth; he went away and became convinced of what had indeed come to pass.

Those who, unable to recognise they are dead, become bewildered and resentful are not in the mainstream of experience but are temporarily unhappy victims in need of rescue from themselves.

That such people, according to these accounts, do not know that they are dead points again to the small amount of pain in the actual experience of dying. Why, it will be asked, are such people not immediately met and reassured by other discarnates? It is probable that they are temporarily so immersed in their recent attitudes and sensations as to be unable to become effectively aware of what is now around them. Once this self-preoccupation passes, they are able to meet new companions and accept their help and good will. Sometimes it is considered best that this first process of re-education is carried out by someone unknown to the survivor. A friendly stranger, perhaps, approaches him. In time the survivor finds this stranger knows a great deal about him and his character. This engages his attention and he is then readier to listen. Later he is likely to find that this is a spiritual teacher appointed to him, at least for the time being. No one can hope to understand the nature of living after death without admitting the principle of help from other beings. This help is available, essential, and, we shall see later, reaches deep into the being of the one helped. It comprises much more than the mere imparting of information.

As would be expected, a joyful meeting with those loved, such as that already quoted, is the most common event described. These meetings, even when with those long and dearly loved, sometimes entail a degree of adaptation in dress and look by those who greet the newcomer to ensure that they are recognised; it takes place in a form well adapted to the newcomer's immediate emotional needs. Helen Salter tells how she was met :

> My parents, A. W. and Margaret, came from regions and appearances beyond my ken and *adopted the old disguises.* These are all in the litter of memory. They have appeared to me, as I remembered them in the earlier years of my life. They brought with them my very old-fashioned home of long ago and its dear, comfortable ugliness, its books, its papers and its flowers, even the photographs that figured in numbers in Victorian sitting-rooms, drawing-rooms, studies. How I am enjoying its dear atmosphere ! I was very tired and it has been so restful to me – imbued as it is with the fragrance of many distant memories. Oh, it will change, I know. Later on – visitors, friends, the setting of another scene in my life.[16]

The key to these experiences, and indeed to many other types of discarnate experience, is an important one. The basic difference in life after death is that the balance between subjective and objective is the reverse of what it is on earth.

Death transports one to what is predominantly a mental world, yet one in which everything is moulded by thought, but seems solid – *seems* is the operative word – much as a table on earth, however active its molecules, seems solid and behaves as if solid. It must be emphasised that much which pictures itself to the newcomer as if it were wholly objective can be really a temporary creation. In Helen's case it was like a projection into space of consciously shaped memories, creating a scene in which the person to be helped can participate : a stage, set for a little drama which has in it both imagination and reality. Helen Salter's parents, in their love for her, recreated the image of her girlhood home not as a private and exclusive thought creation of their own, but as one which they intended to share with her, and into which she could enter as if it were a real room.

Helen's perception of the situation had much more insight than is usual in newcomers, no doubt due to her long participation in psychical research. She shows that it is clearly understood by all present to be a temporary construct, which after a while she would no longer need. This *picture* of a world seemingly much like earth is like a protective coat. It reflects the old familiarities. It is a kindergarten, and the reassurance of its seeming in some ways so like what was left behind is precisely what makes it a kindergarten. In essence it is something to outgrow. To suppose that all this while, since their deaths many years before, these parents have 'lived' in this quasi-physical reproduction of their earth home is quite contrary to what the description itself tells us. It is extremely misleading to take such pictures literally, as some readers are tempted to do even when the account itself painstakingly indicates a different situation.

Surely these much-loved parents are likely, if life after death is no static thing, to have passed through a considerable variety of experiences, which may have much modified their character and possibly their appearance. How, then, best to appear and make themselves known to the new arrival, already bewildered and with much of earth memory still clinging to her? Would she necessarily recognise them at first as they now are? Will they not do better to step back in time, as it were, and reproduce themselves and their clothes in the guise in which she had known them? And why not reproduce besides this image of themselves a picture also of their old home – re-animate an old page of memory for the benefit of the newcomer, to be terminated once its purpose has been served?

The posthumous F. W. H. Myers describes such powers thus :

I have to concentrate my thought for what you might call a moment and I can build up a likeness of myself, send that likeness speeding . . . to a friend, to one that is in tune with me. Instantly I appear before that friend, though I am remote from him, and my likeness holds speech – in thought, remember, not words – with this friend. Yet all the time I control it . . . and as soon as the interview is concluded I withdraw the life of my thought from that image of myself and it vanishes.[17]

Could others share this picture world too, even intrude upon it? Helen Salter said of this creation :

I was back in the old house, enfolded in its past studious contentment. They did not have a number of visitors. It was kept quiet to be a refuge of sheltering peace for me.[18]

Helen Salter presumably could have received 'visitors'. Although much of this temporary resting-place belonged to her past, yet it was also part of her present, in which her parents cherish and protect her, and she responds. Some months later (though she did not say that it took place in this setting) she did state :

You may or may not believe me. But I have met the group of Cambridge scholars for whom we worked so hard, also our old colleagues, Gerald Balfour, Pid, Mrs. Sidgwick, even her brother Arthur and Sir Oliver [Lodge].[19]

At first it may not be particularly easy to accept this idea of a mentally created environment intimately appropriate to one's inner self. Yet in some ways this parallels earth experience. Take one's earth house. It has been physically constructed to the plans of an architect or merely to those of a speculative builder. It reflects the thought of this designer of the physical shell. In the furnishing, to a limited degree, the ideas and feelings of the occupiers show themselves; in the pictures and books, in all the souvenirs which fill it, the story of the occupiers is represented more clearly; and more closely still in the feelings which exist mutually between the occupiers and which create the atmosphere in the house. The sensitive visitor, sensing this composite atmosphere, part sensory, part non-sensory, divines that it is a happy or unhappy house, diligent or idle, conventional or the reverse, selfish or outward-going. These qualities inhere, to some extent, within the house and point to the kind of life led therein.

Now imagine all that is substantial disappearing, the bricks, the furniture, the bric-à-brac, leaving only the mental and emotional images they held for the occupiers, and still filled with their subjective moods, memories and desires which made up the atmosphere of the house. Next imagine that the interest of the builder and architect in the building has disappeared, their work in it done and their attention now elsewhere; as a result their impress is no longer there, and the building is now remembered entirely according to the thoughts and feelings of the occupiers. Yet, as every account agrees, it will *seem* perfectly solid to its occupiers; but it will not live on, like obstinate bricks and mortar, and will vanish as soon as their use for it vanishes. This is a glimpse, perhaps, of how the *immediate* afterworld reflects *its* occupiers, and of how the 'house' which Helen Salter's parents created partook of and was formed by their own nature and memory.

<h1 style="text-align:center">6</h1>

It can clearly be seen then that *accounts given soon after death present a picture much more like life on earth than is really the case.*

This apparent physicality has been the basis of much scorn and misunderstanding by hostile critics. Nevertheless, true experience can be wrapped in illusory appearances. In some respects it is rather like a dream world. The dreams we take to a psychiatrist are not regarded literally, but they point to very important psychological factors in the dreamer. Early discarnate life is not wholly dreamlike but partly resembles it; like dreams it contains rapidly changing imagery; unlike dreams this imagery sometimes becomes stable and anchored for considerable periods, like Helen Salter's home; again, unlike dreams, the imagery is not created wholly by the dreamer, but also by others to help him. In common with important dreams, early discarnate experiences point to and express the mental and emotional situation within the newcomer; other persons, essentially free of the dream themselves, may yet choose to step in and share it for a while, in order to help the newcomer, although their true life lies elsewhere. This is clearly true of Helen Salter's parents. Most important, those who are confined within their after-death dream usually take what is around them to be completely objective. Once they begin to see that it is not so, then they are beginning to be ready to step out of it into a larger world. Helen Salter was exceptional in being aware of this from the first.

Now we will look at some of the ways in which men and women learn, quickly or slowly, to adapt to themselves and to their new environment, and the happiness and pain, the acceptances and refusals which can result.

CHAPTER 6

The Illusion of the Summerland

maya - illusion - Sanskrit

1

Living on earth is bound up with a great deal of illusion, of Maya. William Blake puts it forcibly:

existed in mexico/Central America AD 300-900

> Do what you will, this life's a fiction
> And is made up of contradiction.

As we have seen, such a state of affairs by no means disappears at death. Since humans bring many of their former illusions with them, their insight into the events which now present themselves must be expected also to be tangled up with their limitations. Nevertheless, we are able on earth, even when prey to a good deal of such illusion, to achieve a degree of spiritual growth. After death, as we shall see in later chapters, the situation is similar.

Meanwhile, in the early stages, the traveller faces experiences which gradually enable him to become fully related to the new life around him. The adjustments needed are both of an outward and an inward kind, the latter being by far the more important. He will have to learn about his environment (including incidentally that highly localised part of it, his clothing) and about the present make-up of his own being.

The key to understanding discarnate life is that we are concerned with a number of different levels of consciousness, and that what is true at one level is not necessarily true in the same way at deeper levels. It is often considered necessary for the sake of clarity to describe post-mortem experiences as if they take place in separate areas or 'spheres', and as if these areas are sharply divided off from one another. The real difference, however, has to be seen in terms of expanding consciousness. Discarnate experiences represent an adventure in growth. Like other forms of growth this does not take place in an even and uniform way. Such growth can contain temporarily neglected areas, which must be made good at a later period. A man can advance or retreat within his own consciousness with a motion like a wave on a beach. He can also take byways from which for a long while he can refuse to disentangle himself.

The general direction of his experiences, however, can be stated fairly simply. During earth life men know comparatively little of their true nature. This is partly because they imprison themselves in various illusions, and partly because they succeed in expressing only a comparatively small part of their full being. Many sense that this is so whilst they are still on earth. The purposes of the early, or comparatively early, stages of the next life are first to enable a man to recognise and shake off his illusions, often by continuing to live within them until their illusion becomes clear to him; second, to come to recognise himself in a far more objective way; and third, to discover how to reach and live more fully within those parts of his nature which he had not expressed whilst on earth.

These three stages can roughly be equated with (1) the illusory state known as the Summerland, (2) the judgement, and (3) life in the First, Second and Third Heavens.

2

On earth a great deal of effort has to be expended in order to make an impact upon its material density, rather as the mountaineer can only slowly cut each step before him as he makes his way up the ice slopes. The traveller now has to learn (as Helen Salter's parents had long since done) how he can

transform .the ideoplastic and malleable material he now
encounters. Whilst some continue to take it that the physical
appearances they observe are much as of old, others are more
alert and recognise readily that the 'matter' now surrounding
them is different.

> . . . There are things . . . of the same kind as you see on earth,
> only somehow different. They are real, but you have a sense
> that they are only temporary, that they just belong to that
> first waking stage.
>
> Then you find, and it seems very curious and fascinating,
> that you can change those things by wishing them to change.
> You can only do it with quite small and unimportant things,
> but for instance – you can look at a pine needle on the ground
> where you are sitting, and begin to think of it as a real needle,
> a steel needle, and then it is an ordinary sewing needle and
> you can pick it up.
>
> You can't change big things, you can't change the whole
> scene around you. That is because it is not only your scene,
> it belongs to lots of other spirits too, but you can change
> any little thing, when the change won't affect anybody else.
> Then you begin to realise that all the things around you are
> really thought forms, and that it is arranged like that so as
> to make the transition easy from material life to spirit life.
> You learn a great deal simply by finding out what you can
> change by changing your own thought about it, and what
> remains unaltered however you think about it.
>
> That makes you understand how little belongs to you
> alone so that you can do exactly what you like with it
> individually and how much belongs to the whole concourse
> of spirits of which you are a part.[1]

Thus the Joe of these scripts can alter matter which has been
thought into a pine needle, and convert it into another shape,
but he cannot alter anything which is held in a stronger pattern
of thought than his own. More experienced beings, like Helen
Salter's parents, give to the environment of new arrivals a
stability which it needs in order to make them feel they are in
some place not too different from what they have been used to.

This is recognised in his own way by a Cockney character who says :

> In the distance we see mountains, guv'nor, but they are
> thought mountains, and however far you walk, you never
> come up to them.[2]

The 'mountains' set a limit beyond which the Cockney and those with him cannot stray for the time being. It represents a limit of consciousness, for what lies beyond this pictured barrier is what is beyond their understanding.

> You must remember that his surroundings hereafter are
> limited by his mental and spiritual development up to date.
> He himself is the same as he was when he was here because
> that is the conception of himself that he holds in his mind.
>
> Mind controls all things.
>
> The present margin of the mental consciousness limits the
> present capacity for perception.[3]

It is admittedly hard to visualise a world which has the appearance of being a physical world; which, as all accounts agree, has substance of a kind; and yet which also has the property of reflecting and representing inner thoughts and feelings. It is through refusing to face this difficulty that pictures of the next world are taken to be more materialistic than the accounts themselves say.

Although it is very necessary to emphasise the malleability and ideoplastic nature of this substance, we then run the risk of giving it too Berkeleyan a character. This overemphasis is hard to avoid because as yet we have certainly not received any satisfactory account of how this substance is made up.

The more these records are studied, in fact, the more perplexing sensory matters become. They are continually baffling.

Thus, communicators speak of a 'soul-body'. Rationalists dismiss this phrase as no more than a contradiction in terms. Professor Anthony Flew amusingly calls it a non-tauride bull. If one regards 'soul-body' as a term denoting a centre of consciousness, this too can be said to beg all the questions, for it tells us nothing of *how* such a centre operates, nor of how far something sensory is involved. And yet it may be a starting place, a finger post pointing us in the right direction.

If we make earth experiences the standard by which to judge whether sensory references in the narratives are acceptable, this amounts to requiring post-mortem existence to obey much the same rules as those of our earth body.

This would then make subsequent existence after all much like life on earth; yet this is the very thing other critics condemn. If such a standard is imposed, is this really akin to looking through the wrong end of the telescope? Why should bodily laws as we know them prevail after death, when the absence of a physical body is the one certain thing which makes it different? If we turn the telescope round, we can then at least ponder on whether post-mortem experiences show our physical make-up to have been a limitation, and not belonging to our essence. Mystical experiences on earth transcend the everyday limitations of the senses in just this way. Mystics and post-mortem teachers sometimes tell a strikingly similar story.

Here is a post-mortem account (there are other similar ones):

. . . You are part of the tree, in tune with it; it feeds you and you respond to it in that you recognise it as a reflection of God's love as you are a reflection of God's love. It emits a sound like a beautiful tiny bell, again quite impossible to describe, but you hear it within yourself and respond spiritually. The flowers can dance and sing in their own particular way . . . everything gives you of itself in a conscious overwhelming generosity of joy and you reciprocate, sharing everything around you with this giving and taking.[4]

And here are two experiences on earth:

I was walking on the lawn looking at the masses of flowers in the herbaceous border. As a gardener I was interested in what was coming up into flower; as an artist I was enjoying the combination of colour, light and shade. Suddenly . . . I was 'lifted' into another world. I did not seem to be inside myself though I was still looking normally at the flower border. Everything had become a thousand times more brilliant. Everything had also become transparent. But what was so amazing was . . . that I was not only seeing the colours – I was hearing the colours! Every colour was an indescribably exquisite musical sound, the whole making a harmony that no instruments could produce. I do not know how long this illumination lasted, perhaps not more than a second or two, but as I came back to earth, so to speak, I knew I had been in Reality.

The memory of it has remained vivid and real ever since, and has brought me the greatest happiness and understanding Now I *know*.[5]

I was on the Downs . . . and felt the conditions change. I became aware of faculties which normally I have not at all. I could hear each little blade of grass vibrating and there was harmony in every note. I could see an aura to every flower . . . I seemed to be conscious of being in a quite new world; my material body was forgotten. I felt an inward world of colour, music and scent, and perfect peace and happiness . . . I am sure there is something there with movement, colour and sound, which gives happiness . . . I am really rather an active sort of person . . . All my friends call me extremely practical.[6]

Are these mystical experiences on earth anticipatory, showing by a temporary transcending of physical sensory limitations something of what we shall all experience when we shed these limitations permanently?

3

Clothes form a very good illustration of how outer things can both express and be obedient to an inner thought creation. The process can be very swift.

Some speak of finding themselves naked on arrival after

death, but when a stranger approaches they immediately think of clothes, and then as quickly find themselves clothed in a familiar way. Their 'surround' of clothes is produced by their own mind. Walt Whitman will have clothed himself mentally in a garb his old friend just before death was bound to recognise. Are these clothes, one must ask, real enough to be taken off, folded away, and resumed later on? The probable answer is that they become as 'real' as this only if the wearer believes they are and wishes to make them so. By his need, or imagined need, he takes a share both in their creation and their temporary preservation.

A Swiss, in re-experiencing the keen faculties he had known in his early earth life, with their accompanying sense of well-being, finds himself instantaneously wearing the familiar army uniform which had been his at the time. The uniform will disappear when he alters his consciousness, to be replaced as easily by whatever new garment he imagines. This might become, for instance, a Grecian robe, representing the philosophic and idealistic side of his nature. The 'surround' of clothes is produced by the wearer's own sense of what is fit. It can provide a shelter from what might be thought to be unwelcome scrutiny, as a crab lives in its shell; or it can express an ideal, as in an account of John Ruskin choosing to wear in the next world a beautiful, long sky-blue robe with a girdle; or it can reproduce an illusion as in the finery which some feel is their personal due; or it can be merely a memory habit, the wearing of the form of a garment familiar from earth and felt to be appropriate; or a working tool, as Frances Banks made of her nun's robe.

The nature of man's own substance after death is a more difficult matter. Although many accounts broadly agree, they speak largely in terms of analogy, as in the following account.

> I was a doctor on earth . . . but I had no use for religion or faith healing, or any of those sentimental emotions. . . . I woke up in a hospital. I had died at home and could not think how I'd got there. But it was a most wonderful place. . . . A doctor came over to me. "We shall be glad to teach you all we know". . . . He sat down beside me, and out

of nowhere a diagram appeared showing the organs and arteries of my new body . . . similar in shape to the one I knew, but with . . . digestive organs and so on, of a much simpler kind . . . The digestive organs seemed to be on a rotary system. It looked like one large fly-wheel that drew in from all sides the white and coloured rays, transforming them into energy and *life* such as I am now experiencing.[7]

Man's substance might be expected to be adapted to, and possess something of, the 'material' of the new environment, just as formerly it was adapted to and possessed something of the substance, the 'clay', of earth. After a man sheds his physical body he appears to possess, according to many accounts, a more subtle 'etheric' shape – his 'feeling stuff' or vehicle of consciousness. This shape or pattern, it is said, was also his when on earth, where it played a highly important, though less obvious part behind the scenes. For on this more subtle shape the thoughts and feelings of his earth life gradually impressed themselves, forming his own private think-tank and feeling-tank. Now that the physical body has dropped off, it becomes in turn his outer shape and forms a continuing vehicle in which he lives. However indefinite and speculative these concepts are – a mere label, some will say – the accounts unfailingly point to man still having a shape and one which, for a while at least, enables old friends to recognise him.

The posthumous T. E. Lawrence feels his way to a concept of this solidity :

. . . There has been an unreal quality in my surroundings, and in myself a feeling of shadowy and unsubstantial being. I still miss the weight of my earth body, I suppose, although I should be sorry now to have to drag it about . . . my present body, solid as it seems, is now really composed of a kind of matter which on earth I thought of as 'emotion'. This 'feeling stuff' is now exterior to the real me and has no physical drag to slow down its activity. Hence the frightening release of emotional energy and the impossibility of masking it.[8]

4

Consciousness, it is clear, does not expand at an even rate; it can intensify and then diminish again. Those who have a degree of spiritual maturity, who quickly accept the fact of their death, and are at once eager to learn, can experience such a temporary intensification very quickly.

> Remarkable is the impression of *time,* which is not measured in the same way as on earth. Thus it seemed to me that I had spent at least several months in the 'Elysian Fields' – or what I took for them. It was a state of serene bliss, of complete relaxation.
> In the beginning I was more or less conscious of the presence of loved and familiar faces . . . it seemed to me, as though all around me there were large and fresh fields covered with flowers. I was constantly surrounded by this golden haze. But I rather felt things, than actually saw them . . . I saw a great many things that were new to me. I walked about, met many an old friend and some new ones. So that I had the impression of having lived here already for a long time.
> Gradually I was overcome by weariness. I wanted a regenerating bath. . . .
> When my attention turned towards you again, I realized that *this lapse of time, so long and full, corresponded to three or four terrestial days.*[9]

This vista of Pauchard's can perhaps be compared with wandering around a college or university when joining the other students, before the hard work of term-time begins.

5

Pauchard's intense nature was very soon ready for work again. Many others need a much longer and more gradual period of adjustment, average people who are slower to discover the depth of experience open to them. At an early stage of this new life these usually declare that they are in what is often named the Summerland.

Here an ordinary, decent man begins to feel at home on finding an environment seemingly similar to that which he knew on earth, where he meets friends and relatives and even finds a replica of the house he desires. All this expresses his present, if only temporary, inner need. A communication from F. W. H. Myers describes it thus:

Nearly every soul lives for a time in the state of illusion. The large majority of human beings when they die are dominated by the conception that substance is reality, that their particular experience of substance is the only reality. They are not prepared for an immediate and complete change of outlook. They passionately yearn for familiar though idealised surroundings. Their will to live is merely to live, therefore, in the past. So they enter that dream I call illusion-land. For instance, Tom Jones, who represents the unthinking man in the street, will desire a glorified brick villa in a glorified Brighton . . . He naturally gravitates towards his acquaintances, all those who were of a like mind. But he is merely dreaming all the time, or, rather, living within the fantasy created by his strongest desires on earth.[10]

Such persons have no very severe defects to overcome as a result of their life on earth. In the main they will have accepted with little question the habits and customs around them. To them, moral standards were largely a form of respectability and of easy comfort; they did not have the stature to face great issues, and passed through life largely as satisfactory citizens, but asleep in part of their being.

It is perfectly possible for a man to imprison himself just as firmly to his Summerland environment as he formerly did to his earth environment. For this continuing existence forms the world of himself, writ just a little larger, and, since men resemble one another very much, only a very small portion of it will be unique to himself. The greater part of what the ordinary man seeks around him represents a commonality existence, shared with others at the same level of awareness.

6

In the Summerland many declare that they find that their new 'body' or vehicle of consciousness gradually comes to resemble the one which was theirs on earth when in their youthful prime. This too is a condition of mind. They find that they need no longer carry around with them the concept of an old, tired and imperfect body – the illusion of age. When they claim to be growing younger every day, and to be growing back to their prime, this must not be looked upon as some sort of physiological miracle. It is simply a change of consciousness to which the feeling-self adapts.

But on earth different people feel in their prime at different times. To some, youth is the prime, to be ever after looked back upon with regret for its loss; to most, maturity; to a comparative few it is old age which brings ease and contentment. At certain stages of their life some will have met with wounding experiences or felt ill at ease and inadequate; they now for a while continue to associate this private experience with the particular age when it occurred. Therefore some prefer to wear a mask of age, rather than the cloak of youth or maturity assumed by others, because they cling to the time which brought them most happiness. To such, acclimatisation proves slow. Eventually such blockages become removed as earth discomfitures fade and their consequences upon the individual nature are overcome. There will then be no need to cling to a certain age.

Some people remain caught up in their old life pattern because of former skills. They find it possible to help people still on earth and learn how to do this.

. . . A doctor here . . . has become so linked up with his work, that he cannot resist from exercising his profession.

He works chiefly through clairvoyants and is perfectly happy to see his treatments continued. It is now over fifty years that he carries on his work . . . he has not even taken the time to get interested in anything else. Once I asked him whether he had not had certain experiences – pleasant or disagreeable – very different to those on earth . . . He answered half-surprised, half absent-minded 'No !'[11]

This doctor's unchanged attitude has more than one aspect and is probably not quite as admirable as it sounds. It may hide a deep inability to face up to other sides of his character, so that in choosing to confine himself to his better and perfectly sincere sides he is refusing to take the disciplinary path which alone will lead him to the wider future which will then become available to him. His work provides service to others, but could be as well a refuge from himself, and on that account a more limited service than need be. A respectable life is, in itself, no passport to spiritual advancement. The doctor, in spite of all his service, may yet lack one part of the root of the matter, which less laudable persons quickly gain.

An old man came over here after an earth life that was by no means exemplary. He was a thief who had killed a man during one of his expeditions, and as soon as he arrived here, he met his victim. He did not know how to express his sorrow, but the victim had no ill feeling and told him that he was grateful for his release from a wretched earth life . . . He set to work to teach the old man that he must atone for his bad life, but that the punishment was automatic and not vindictive. After a time, the murderer and his victim became fast friends, and made progress together. It is not always the apparently good people who get on quickly over here.[12]

The Hunt tapes include interesting records of crude self-applied limitations, the majority of them in persons of comparatively slender mental and emotional substance. A character states that he lived in the eighteenth century, naming himself as Sir Rupert Benton. He then proceeds to give a description of this past life of his and of its aristocratic setting. Some time later, many weeks onward, he comes to confess that on earth he had in truth only been the servant, the very envious servant, of the real Sir Rupert Benton. We see him finding his very slow way towards reality through this impersonation enjoyed and paraded before others. But why has it taken from the eighteenth century for this casting-off to be completed? Why do not others, kindly in purpose, disillusion him? It is because his fantasy, and this is important, remains his to accept as long as he wills to; if he prefers to believe it – even if in one part of his being he knows it is otherwise – no one can make him step outside it. Similarly the doctor can continue his ministrations just as long as it suits him. The two things certain about such illusions are their ultimate disappearance and their owner's inalienable right to continue them meanwhile.

Others support very different illusions from that of 'Sir Rupert Benton'. A group of brothers of the Celtic Church of the ninth century, former monks of Lindisfarne, speak of their life in the 'etheric' world.[13] They too have been caught in a dream of their own, and for a very much longer period than 'Sir Rupert Benton'; it is a comparatively harmless dream, very much a continuation of their old earth life, which after all was the life they then chose and for which they renounced much else. They tell of the abbey, a duplicate of the one they knew on earth; they tell, even, of the flocks they believe they still tend, and theirs must be almost the only account where money is spoken of as still in active circulation after death. These brethren look on their life as a loyal and patient waiting for the second coming of Christ on earth. When some of their members leave them, the remainder sorrow at this infidelity, but of course the absentees are really the brethren who have made progress, casting off this enclosing illusion and going on to a wider life.

These are instances of persons who have chosen to step apart and isolate themselves, in various ways, from the forward-going processes which others face up to earlier, whether eagerly or reluctantly. Each can refuse help; he is free to do so, but the result inevitably will be to chain himself a little more firmly to his past. This is what 'Sir Rupert Benton' did; and so, if we believe it, does the figure of Henry VIII in *A Tudor Story*, displaying what to his earth listener, Canon Pakenham-Walsh, is a truly terrible temper, still claiming that his monarchy must be accepted by all around him and refusing to throw it off and accept plain manhood. To use the metaphor of a prison suggests an iron necessity, and so it is in the case of rebellious and wilfully selfish persons. For the ordinary, decent, willing person the bars of necessity, though equally effective, are more of silk than of iron, but will hold him just as fast.

Very unpleasant conditions – what might be called the Winterland – which are also illusory, though in a different way, surround those whose life was one of coldly selfish feelings and of self-imposed isolation. After death – and also before it, as many enlightened persons have found – experience is not to be sought *because* it is pleasant, nor shortened *because* painful. Each needs to be accepted for what it teaches. In the lower areas – it is almost impossible to avoid these geographical concepts – men discover their actual self to which on earth they preferred to remain largely blind. Now they can no longer avoid their real selves; it is unpleasant where they are, because *they* are unpleasant. Whilst deploring their surroundings, they often insist upon remaining there, for many were headstrong on earth; having refused to face up to themselves then, it is the harder to learn to do so now. A very selfish man is often depicted as finding himself in a rocky landscape, surrounded by a grey, dark mist. How, then, it may be asked, is this a representation of familiar places on earth, for many selfish men used their life to acquire a rich and splendid house and a staff to surround them. This former earth setting is not now reproduced because it does not represent the reality of such a man's internal state. The ordinary man who led a pleasant if unadventurous life finds largely familiar-looking surroundings because these do, in their way, still represent him and his limitations. The outer and the inner man were not too different so he is able to ease himself gradually into more demanding realities. But what a selfish man built around him on earth and believed to be his is so different from what his real character now reflects in his surroundings that an extremely unpleasant shock faces him.

But it will be asked, how can it be possible for only *one* environment to represent fully and accurately a state of being which, in every man, will be a blend of good and bad? To a degree a man can indeed move around from one level of consciousness to another; each level will seem like a separate 'landscape'; he can have a foot in several, if he will, provided, but only provided, that part of him is attuned to each. However, his own nature may make him almost completely bound to a particular landscape for a while. If a man's nature was mild and pleasant, inertia is likely to keep him in his illusion-land. Others have to remain in Winterland, unpleasant though it is, because they are unable even temporarily to leave off being driven by the passions which placed them there. They cannot register a more pleasant landscape if their own character lacks response to the human qualities which such a landscape reflects; they are at present, as it were, tone-deaf to it.

Frances Banks thus describes the Winterland:

There are also Hells though certainly differing from the physical hells and everlasting fiery torments of man's warped imagination. There are . . . confining states of misery; dark, repressing and as real as the tortured consciousness of the dweller therein makes them. Yet these hells are not eternal. The man (or woman) in these mental torments need stay there no longer than his desires keep him. He is free to resist the hatreds, cruelties, lusts of his lower nature which he has retained from his earth life and which are keeping him in dark dungeons amid like-minded inhabitants. He can always choose to follow the Light of Love, Forgiveness and Harmony and always there are souls ready to help, to guide, to comfort and to assist.

No soul is ever left comfortless unless he wishes it.

That sounds like a paradox, but then much that we learn here is very different from the teachings of man, even good men who are limited in their ideas. Existence on earth is a state of living in a thought world, illusory and much more restricted and enclosed by the glamorous web of matter. Beyond physical death the thought world is more apparent and certainly far more potent in its effects. Cause and Effect is still the Law on this plane of astral matter, as it is on earth.

The Shadow Land is a very real place indeed; a gloomy murk covers it to which one has to become accustomed; squalid dwellings inhabited by unhappy, tormented beings who jeer and mock and pursue their warped existences. Sometimes these poor souls live in hatred and rebellion, sometimes in apathy and sometimes with a fierce denial that there is any other state of existence possible.[14]

The temporary self-induced tragedy of these people lies in the deep hold their selfish qualities have taken upon them. The result is a spiritual isolation; the traveller hides from his fellow beings because he hates them or fears them or is selfishly uncaring. They are repellent to him as he also is to them, because their qualities of selfishness are similar.

The miser, the misanthrope, the unending critic, the cold intellectual, the selfish aristocrat, the ruthless tycoon – these put around themselves an encrustation, bringing about a self-imposed isolation which prevents true contact with other beings. These are the people who in their lives have moved backwards, and the slopes of recovery they now face are correspondingly steep. Later on they will encounter the heavy extra burden of remorse, and of being obliged to secure forgiveness from every person they have wronged. The burden is heavy, as many accounts of their extrications declare.

Sin is in part error or ignorance; a diversion, a misunderstanding of truth, undeveloped good. Selfishness, pride, and independence of God are the roots of all evil and the beginnings of sin. Thence come dissension, strife, and conflict. . . . If hell is simply a mental condition within one's self, if it is self-exclusion from God, from the Father's heart and home, then men make their own hell. How long will it last? As long as they exclude God and his infinite grace from their lives. It is not God's will that any should perish.[15]

No exile lasts a day beyond the term the prisoner himself chooses to put upon it. Once he truly wishes no longer to continue thus, simultaneously the fringes of the next area of consciousness begin to present themselves to him. The landscape to which he then finds his way is not quite so dark, rocky, stony. The mist lightens, perhaps grass appears underfoot instead of rock, a few flowers may show and after a while a shaft of sunshine. Literal descriptions of such landscapes, though they truly describe what such unfortunate souls see and experience, do not always stress the important part of the story; that the outer represents the inner. These seemingly objective obstacles and hateful surroundings are the prisoner's own mind made objective. In a kind of way, they can be said to be waking dreams. The dream, as with important dreams on earth, gives information about his inner self which the outer being has refused and censored. It is certainly not easy to understand this process of life being turned, as it were, inside out; the familiar balance of earth life reversed. But this is the basic situation always described.

If, then, such landscapes reflect the minds of those who inhabit them, does the landscape remain when they have left it? It remains as long as minds of similar cast come along with a similar inner landscape for it to reflect. If there were no such minds, there would be no such landscapes; the inner world met after death is subjective enough for that. Once these prisoners have departed, its basic plasticity of substance would be available to reflect minds of different quality.

If the self-imposed isolation is deliberately continued, and with it the delaying of any remorse, then those who are in this same sorry condition remain grouped together, unable to help one another, each in the same prison without bars. Here they may continue for long periods, refusing help, sometimes with anger and contempt towards those who in their self-won freedom attempt to reach and rescue them.

To enter these areas fills rescuers with a deep sense of distress; these helpers, sensitive men and women, can themselves become affected and drawn into some of the purblind emotions they seek to lift from others, and if they remain too long in this area they declare they can, to some extent, be temporarily overcome by them. For the price to be paid in order to reach these minds is to lower their own consciousness and concepts to a level acceptable to, and capable of being understood by, those they hope to rescue. Evil is powerful at its own level, and clearly a rescuer needs sterner qualities than those of the self-congratulatory do-gooder. To compassion, insight must be added, and a ready power of wit to negotiate and to find some chink in the armour of isolation of these prisoners : some area of good – and of course there always is such an area – in the most depraved, where they can find a response and then attempt to help their self-growth, however slight.

Eventually, the self-obstacles will be overcome, but in some cases it takes the equivalent of what on earth would be a very long time indeed.

Time, however, does not matter, nor that some delays, like that which Henry VIII imposed on himself, can apparently last the equivalent of hundreds of years. The most difficult cases are said to be when a person either disbelieves completely any possibility of life after death, or accepts it but believes that it will only come about after the last trump has sounded. Both types of self-victim are described as being in a form of sleep, refusing, in some strange part of their being, to allow their consciousness to function. Surely, we ask, there must be some mode of access to whatever part of the mind has made this choice and imposed upon itself insensibility to all that is around it? It is like a coma, but a self-chosen one which for long refuses to respond to any external pressures. Absolute respect for the law of free will is observed and somehow the coma has to be penetrated to bring about a change. Those who would help say this can be extremely difficult. It is, however, a striking instance both of the respect for free will and of how deep subjectivity can go.

7

To return to the ordinary, decent person in the Summerland. We have seen that really, in spite of the lyrical descriptions sometimes given, it is an area of limitation. Myers calls it Lotusland, or Illusionland, because it is based upon a reconstruction of earth memories of enjoyment and upon an expectation of reward. If a symbol is sought which will describe the state of a man who thinks he has already arrived in heaven, and at such easy cost, an armchair in front of one's own porch would not be a bad image.

Woven into this, however, is another, somewhat deeper aspect, not based on earth memories but upon the hopes, longings and ideals which had lain deep in the traveller's heart but which he had never been able to express in his outer life; the parts of his nature to which life had brought no fulfilment. This too must now come to expression, and its precise worth will be shown to him in this new, kindly environment in which old earth obstacles do not exist. There is now nothing to stop him, and everything to help him, to give to his ideals the expression which had eluded him on earth. But this second phase of the Summerland also falls short of reality. If this is accepted, some of the difficulties in the concept of the Summerland disappear, including the perfectly sound and correct view held by many sceptics that the felicity seemingly described is too easy, has not been earned.

So now a man's interior dreams are put to the test by being granted to him. All his earth wishes come true, or so it seems. At first, all is wonder and delight. It seems he has indeed found himself. But, this easy conquest made, there is an aftermath of a kind not quite expected. What he has now drawn around him in an idealised form, and shares with others, is limited, in this mental world, to the actual extent of reality his imagination can impart to it. In his uncritical way, he delights in it. After a while, like his own earth nature, it proves to be insufficient. There is more to the human spirit than the possession of such enjoyments. As the post-mortem Myers says, there is one greater misfortune than the non-realisation of the heart's desire, and that is its realisation. It is a cloud-cuckoo-land of the well-meaning man, and is no more than this because nearly all of it is fundamentally selfish. Even the pleasure of his relationships revolves around his own well-being. It is the land of heart's desire; but the heart of man, as Kipling says, is small. Allowed to create his idea of heaven, would not his creation be expected to be as limited as is the man himself?

The purpose of this phase is to bring to an end all these personal emotions and thoughts which were wasted because out of them no spiritual harvest was garnered on earth. He will not be able to carry them with him later on into the more demanding subsequent phases of living where, at last, he will be concerned with his true spiritual harvest, those qualities he did fulfil and so built into a permanent part of his own being. So in the end the self-created enjoyments which he has been experiencing lose their meaning and savour. What at first seemed so desirable and satisfying (and of which meanwhile he may have given descriptions to friends on earth through a medium) now proves to be an illusion. A sense of stagnation descends upon him, he tires of his own felicity, for something is stirring within him which tells him that he is not satisfied, that there are hidden areas of life ahead of him.

> You will find that the gratification of your desires quickly palls, but at least you have the pleasure of it before this happens . . . No, it does not last. It is not meant to. But you will have it as long as you want it. Nobody will hurry you . . . You yourself will be sated with it first.[16]

Once the traveller accepts that these pleasures have no further meaning for him, he becomes willing to let them go. Now he is ready to move on, for in the afterlife every step that is taken must be a step earned even if, as in these early stages, the earning comes about through a casting-off. It is a clearing of the decks to enable him to grow into the deeper part of his nature. He comes to see his own complacency. 'Eternal progress open to all' is a principle of the Spiritualist religion, where it is apt to be considered as a right, like social security. But of course it has to be earned. No one content with such terms is going to get himself very far in the lands after death – no moving staircase is provided to carry him upward!

Except possibly for a brief space for readjustment, the easy-going enjoyment of Summerland is not for eager souls of sterner temperament because its experiences would already be worth-less to them. They bypass it or, to put it more accurately, they come to the next life having already lived on earth at a level of consciousness beyond that at which such an existence could ensnare them. It holds no necessity for them, hence they do not meet the experience. It is not for those who, in Milton's phrase, 'scorn delight and live laborious days'. Others of more easy going and unchallenging character need it as a comparatively gentle way of becoming shorn of their illusions of what makes up bliss. The Summerland, then, far from being the heaven with which some equate it, represents a comparatively lowly experience, but one necessary to the majority of people.

8

It would not be wise, however, to take everything in the Summer-land as empty illusion. It is real in the exhilaration the traveller feels in living without the heaviness of a physical body, his 'gross and muddy vesture of decay'. This absence of physical illness and deterioration brings a degree of freedom. He is beginning to discover that his interior self, his vehicle of consciousness, is far more important than the physical body into which it had been confined. He has access to his thoughts and feelings in a much more unimpeded way and in an environment much less clogg-ing and resistant.

The Summerland is also real enough in providing early lessons in the use of the creative powers which lie in his thoughts and emotions, as evidenced in the malleable nature of his new environment. He is educating himself in powers he will learn to control in due time. And of course there is truth in the whole process of casting off veils in his nature which will later on lead to the discovery of his true inner being.

The Summerland is also a foreshadowing of later surroundings. It is described as a land of sunlight. Here it must be said that the sunlight, the water, the landscape, the moving stream, the woods and hills which are described must not be regarded too literally. Myers found them to be brought about by those he calls the Wise Ones, who create an environment appropriate to their charges but more skilfully than these could do it for themselves. The environment resembles a pictorial representation, an artist's composition – like Helen Salter's drawing-room but on a vaster scale. These landscape-like surroundings are meaningful images, as an artist's design is meaningful. It is like a less obdurate form of nature, one not heartless, witless, as Housman declares, but somehow imbued with intelligent purpose. Water there is said to bring a sense of deeply vivifying refreshment. Fruits, too, unusual fruits, are described, which can in some way be imbibed and which, too, produce this sense of vivification.

There is no need to eat, because there is no physical body which needs food, though old habits may bring about a sensation of needing food. But this error is used for teaching, for, even when thought of as physical food, the vivification it brings represents a momentary participation in what, in essence, is a slightly higher level of consciousness. It is this which the Summerland apple or peach is likely to produce and of which it is a symbol.

When you first arrive here, however, the routines of eating and drinking and sleeping are too firmly established to be eliminated at one fell swoop. So if you think you need to sleep . . . you sleep for as long as you want. If you think you need to eat, then you eat your fill. There are no excretory organs in our bodies . . . When I drink water it just diffuses itself throughout my system, and that's that! In other words, it's converted into energy. If I see a beautiful apple tree with bright red apples on it, I can reach up and pick one off . . . It has the effect of recharging our batteries.[17]

It is as if these representations bear within them in a living way a message from the deeper consciousness which created them. Thus man in the Summerland can learn from these things; he is surrounded by events which point to a larger reality. There is a gradual overlapping into his consciousness, a gentle infiltration and preparation. He is learning to throw off some illusions, but meanwhile he is also learning something for use in his own future.

In time his complacence is shaken in another way for he finds that, though he is happy with his companions, certain of these disappear. They have removed themselves from his layer of consciousness. They have gone on, for they realise their life now needs to be lived more strenuously.

It must be emphasised that a great deal of this post-mortem experience is often very gradual, resembling the process of growth and change on earth and in humans themselves. Sojourn in the Summerland need not end through a sudden step, but as its necessity gradually recedes. It is probable that there is an overlapping of experiences some of which are a preparation for life in the first heaven. On earth some of us meet decisive experiences, when the face of life changes overnight. But much more, quite as decisively in the end, takes place almost insensibly, so gradual is it; the changes, for instance, which come about in long and intimate relationships, and in our own growing and ageing. So after death many move gradually from one experience to another and grow in the process, move up from one level of consciousness to the next, but also give attention, as on earth, to more than one task at a time, for growth of consciousness is often uneven, strong in one area, hesitant in another.

With this in mind it becomes easier to see how individual idiosyncrasies can continue to exist, how experiences which all must eventually undergo can come to different people, or be chosen by them, in quite different order; and how even after death many remain within some psychological hang-up or refusal, and baulk at experiences perfectly open to them.

> People who don't like change find it somewhat bewildering at first and so avoid experiencing much that they could enjoy. 'The small cage habit' applies even here. Probably the most obvious 'cages' are those created by narrow sectarian beliefs.
> That is where the Artist has the pull over the conventional religionist – there are no barriers to be overcome. The negative approach, the perpetual 'thou shalt not', is very hampering.[18]

Once he has put the Summerland behind him, the traveller, as we have seen, has thereby made himself more ready to meet experience at a deeper level. What he next finds is likely to bring him certain surprises.

CHAPTER 7

The Judgement

1

The traveller is now able to face the process of finding how he has become what he is as a result of how he dealt with the experiences he underwent on earth, which have gradually made up his present feeling-thinking being. He has to accept himself as the man whom *he* has created, and to realise that he cannot conceal his real nature from others. The corollary is that he gradually comes to see the need to change himself. He faces a quickening process of becoming aligned to living more nakedly within himself. Gradually he will realise the value (or lack of value) of his own stock-in-trade; deprived now of his earth possessions he has to rely on the interior possessions he has brought with him – his character, his memories, his powers of thinking and feeling and perceiving. These are what he has to support him in an environment whose laws he does not yet understand and which, he will find, will gradually test his attributes to the full.

Death, far from having been a final event, is indeed proving to be merely an introduction. It involves this somewhat painful process of coming to know himself as never before. So it is by no means only to his environment that he has to adjust, but to his own self. His day, or rather days, of reckoning, both for good and for bad, lie ahead. In the reckoning, he will also find his rightful place in the new world around him.

2

Thus in due course, everybody meets the experience known as the judgement. Many communications, and not only Christian-oriented ones, describe this judgement; it is a highly important event for the individual, which will occupy him over what is the equivalent of a considerable period of time and will have decisive effects upon him. As we have seen, it does not necessarily take place immediately or closely after death. The full sum of his life is not thrust at once upon a man willy-nilly; it will come about when he is ready for it.

In a sense the illusions of the Summerland, the isolation of Benton and the Celtic brethren, and the harsh experiences of the Winterland are all part of a judgement, for they are ways of a man coming to know himself. But they also have within them a deep refusal to face the self : the person is not yet ready. The judgement now to be spoken of, once embarked on, cannot be gainsaid and will proceed to its conclusion. It is entirely objective and calls on the one judged for an equally objective acceptance of what it discloses.

After-death judgement is normally thought of as a retro-spective thing, and of course it points to consequences of actions carried out on earth. The past is irrevocable, certainly; however, its consequences are not final, they can be overcome. Therefore it would be equally true to regard the judgement as a stock-taking, as a result of which a man discovers limitations created by past acts or omissions which have put part of him into a self-prison. It must not be supposed, of course, that all the factors in his judgement are negative ones. A man finds there his positive qualities too and, just as the negative factors make for limitation, the positive ones make for him a free pathway into his future; they are expansive and liberating.

Thus there is this important difference from the once-for-all judgement pictured in so many world religions. Though it is none the less decisive, its meaning is very different. Its purpose

is not punishment, but education. It is non-vengeful, and beneficent in its effects. In this judgement a man is introduced to a
precise record of every outer and inner event of his life on earth.
It is frequently said that this process is carried out by oneself, and
in essence this is true. But since the traveller is likely to have
misjudged himself, perhaps very seriously, whilst on earth, how
does he acquire the insight to make the judgement correctly?
To see himself as he really is and was itself requires enhanced
powers of judgement and of self-analysis.

Two new factors, therefore, emerge. The first is that some
change must come about in him, to produce or make possible
this required deeper insight. This will partly be stimulated by
the unexpected information which will reach him in the judgement, through the intimate picture of his past life which is
presented. The second factor is that he will be helped further by
discussing his situation with a teacher allotted to him. This
instruction is of a rather painful kind. Judgement is a complex
process and certainly not carried out in a uniform way. For
temperaments vary, and some are unable to take as much
truth, or take it as quickly, as others can; like some horses they
first refuse their fences as too steep to surmount. They are free
to refuse them and to continue to canter round an earlier part of
the course, but in the end they must face them. Their concepts
of what is good and evil will need to change and to grow too, and
to grow needs time, or the equivalent of time in the afterworld.
The posthumous Conan Doyle says: 'A man does not drop into
a honey pot when he dies.'

W. T. Stead is equally forthright:

At first there is nothing done but what is both helpful and
comforting – later there is a refining process to be gone
through. . . .

On being established here, in the Real World, each one is
interviewed by one of the Advanced Spirit Instructors and the
whole record of earth is discussed and analysed. Reason,
motive and result. The full and detailed record contains everything, there is nothing overlooked, and this is the time for
paying the bill. Each is interviewed alone, and there is a

minute analysis of all events, acts and thoughts. Then there is the making good to be gone through, the sum total to be paid . . . for all our thoughtlessness and our unkind acts and words – all that have had direct results must be paid for.[1]

Communicators clearly find difficulty in conveying this experience of judgement in all its depth, so they frequently make use of simplified pictures and symbols to help us to understand. Hence it is often said that a panorama is shown of all that took place in earth life or that it is represented as if it were on a television screen. The point is that in some manner the traveller is shown every single event in his life as it really was and not as he thought it had been. The record is made straight wherever he misunderstood it. But there is more; besides his own deeds and the thoughts and feelings connected with them, he is also now obliged actually to experience within himself the thoughts and feelings, the pains and pleasures which his actions caused in the lives of other people; exactly what he caused them to feel he, in turn, feels in himself now. This is a surprising and very disconcerting event.

The judgement gradually shows that his present moral stature narrows his horizon somewhere. This principle already exists on earth when we find ourselves facing moral decisions which earlier weaknesses of character have made too difficult, for which we have now become unwilling to pay the required price. So we settle for something easier and thereby further blunt the perception which could make more difficult choices possible in the future. In making the easier choice we have made ourselves smaller. The effects of this become more evident after death.

The panorama is usually spoken of as a single and inevitable event, but this is almost certainly an oversimplification. There are descriptions of another panorama which appears immediately after death, or during clinical death, from which the person later recovers (see p. 34 above). It takes place at great speed, is in forward time sequence, and is viewed with emotional detachment. This however appears to be a different and lesser event. Some pass into death in a deep slumber or after a coma, and in returning to consciousness after death there is often a further period akin to drowsiness and sleep, and it is hard to be sure if all experience this vision. Rudolf Steiner says that all men do so.

> The peculiarity of this tableau is that as long as it remains in the form in which it appears immediately after death, all the subjective experiences of the man during his life are expunged . . . The joys and sorrows connected with the pictures of the past life are not present. The human being confronts this memory-tableau as objectively as he confronts a painting; . . . in an astonishingly brief span of time man sees all the detailed events of his life.[2]

This is an obscure area of description. It is clear however that full judgement involves a total participation in its consequences. There is nothing detached about it.

Since all one's available equipment is needed to face the judgement, it makes sense when it is described as taking place only after the traveller has become adjusted to his new life. This time the sequence takes place in backward time order. Rudolf Steiner endorses this. In this way, after re-experiencing his past, the traveller can then be shown the earlier seeds he had planted which brought about these events; their causal sequence is made clear.

Most people need to have the sequence, or part of it, repeated several times before they can absorb it all. It can be a very severe experience. Ivy Northage's teacher describes it in this way:

> How can I tell you or describe my sensations during that frightful ordeal? Imagine yourself drenched with cold perspiration and feeling that horrible sensation that fear brings. So, I think, would most people be affected. Everything was shown to me and I saw how easily I could have avoided this or that, how simple it would have been to hold out a helping hand here or there, how easy it would have been if I had made myself find time for that! I wanted to weep and could not. I had no means of expressing my most frightful anguish

or the terrible feeling with which I watched my crimes, for
they looked like crimes in that intensified appreciation that is
relative to spiritual wholeness. I watched and I watched! You
do not get any mitigation.[3]

Pauchard's account is a most telling one. In his case purgation
was readily faced very soon after death. He speaks of *scoriae*, an
interesting word with two separate meanings. To excoriate is to
remove the outer covering, and this is precisely what this
panorama does: it removes all the comfortable padding which
people use to justify their actions and hide their real motives.
The other meaning is to flay, and flaying is a painful process.
Pauchard was a very honourable and conscientious man, yet
he now found aspects within himself which he had failed to
recognise on earth.

Every one of us, no matter who he may be, has at the bottom
of his being a layer of dregs, of which he is not aware. I did
not know how true that was until I came here. 'Purgatory' is
not a fancy, it is a reality. We are good people, you and I, and
when coming here I expected to find only glory and delight,
but after the first feeling of liberation has passed we are
brought . . . directly face to face with the various departments
of our I . . . I assure you it is then – and then only – that
one learns what self-knowledge means and it is not difficult to
draw the conclusions. You cannot even imagine all the revela-
tions that result from such objective encounters with our 'I'
when seen under . . . different aspects. There are some very
unpleasant moments to pass through, I can assure you.[4]

During Pauchard's strenuous purgation, he describes an
experience which is not described in most purgation stories but
which may have been the best way for him to recognise the
truth. Less desirable qualities of his own are shown to him, as
if independent objective forms. They are a kind of thought form.
These meet him; and because when he was on earth he sub-
mitted to these qualities they thereby gain a certain power over
him, from which he now has to learn to free himself.

. . . It would seem that, according to each individual, things happen in a slightly different way. In my case, the curious thing was that while walking all by myself along a lonely path, *I was attacked by* wasps – or something of that kind – which *threatened* to sting me.

A Voice, like thunder, said to me :

'Well, you cannot complain. For if they had stung you, what would have become of you?'

And suddenly I realized that this was connected with all *irritations*, all the thoughts of *criticism*, which I had passively borne while on earth. If I had nourished them, the wasps would have stung me. If I had chased them away, there would have been no wasps![5]

Each traveller finds in his soul such lacks, such disabilities, which claim a power over him which prevents him from moving forward; but these might be presented to another in quite a different way, suited to his own particular cast of temperament.

Judgement, it must again be emphasised, has to wait until a man is sufficiently able to face up to it. Those in the Winterland, because they bitterly resent their condition as unjust, would be quite unready to accept all that their panorama, in its total justice, will show them. In their obstinacy they would remain inwardly blind and unresponsive to it.

Purgation is thus no simple matter of credits versus debits; it is a matter of one's qualities, parts of one's very self, which have encrusted the rest of the nature, or have grown up like a wall around it, or have spread within like a cancer; or good qualities which one has mutilated. These are the wounds which the soul must now find out how to heal, qualities which have to be regrown into a different, more positive shape. The cleansing process necessary after the judgement is not achieved automatically through perception of the faults; it requires subsequent hard work upon them. Self-correction can be very painful, as T. E. Lawrence found :

. . . For the first time I was beaten, not by anything exterior – that can happen to anyone – but by an intimate revelation of what was within. I was reduced to a state . . . [where] pride slunk out of sight. Eventually I have regained some balance but only by . . . painfully accepting myself as I am; a mess, a travesty of what I might have been . . . All experiences here are tried out on the quick of the being and in their keenness and piercing reality are beyond anything it is possible to feel on earth. My emotions still shake me dangerously and I have to learn also to take the emotional impact of other beings with equanimity . . . Relations with people, when nothing can be hidden, become a high art requiring control and a larger sympathy than is ever needed on earth where its absence can usually be covered by the conventional word or action. It really amounts to this, that one is not safe until all the twisted, negative emotions are cleared out of one. Then it will be possible to live fearlessly and freely.[6]

By the time the judgement is reached, passions and defects, as T. E. Lawrence so disconcertingly discovered, reveal them-selves in the etheric body for others to see. So a man now experiences in a more intense form the character he brought over from earth, under conditions in which its real nature becomes readily evident. The aftermath of judgement, the time of purgation or Purgatory, to use the Roman Catholic term, is not entirely painful, for the judgement will also show his good side. That which is realistic and serious in him will already be willing to face up to what lies ahead. These parts of his nature will help to speed up the process of his disentanglement from error and misconception. He will be able to use his good quali-ties to help him overcome the rest. But he can never excuse the evil by putting the good in the scales to balance it. The evil remains what it is, until he weeds it out. He finds himself saddled with himself, with the good and the bad alike. Discarnate life during purgation is still variegated and mixed, much as it is on earth. Within the folds, as it were, of his struggle, from time to time he will glimpse what the best part of him can perceive from a step higher up his own Jacob's ladder, though he will not yet be able to retain the vision permanently. He will be obliged to relapse into the remainder of his nature. The traveller has these periods of purging and of respite, in accordance with his own pattern of temperament, turning his attention from one department of his being to another, working now on one factor in himself and now on another.

> this consciousness which is called 'Purgatory', *is not a continuous state* which goes on till the last 'scoria' has been burnt . . . Experience, . . . mine and that of many others, shows that this state *comes and goes*, takes place and passes, one does not know how or when.[7]

The traveller will not be able to move on completely to new 'environments' or areas of consciousness until he has fully worked out what has been hampering him on other levels; he can only temporarily expand his being towards what will be more completely his later on. For quite a while he will continue to carry around a number of sides of himself as he does on earth.

3

The judgement then is best considered as a composite happening, in the course of which various aspects of reality become expressed. Under one aspect it can be regarded as a sequence of events, the first part of which is enacted on earth; the full consequences continue, but only because fully seen later at the deeper levels of consciousness to which the 'panorama' introduces a man. Under another aspect it is a living demonstration of moral forces in the universe playing upon and influencing a human being in order that he can learn to co-operate harmoniously with these; under another aspect still it is the Divine Will expressing itself with infinite justice, patience and love towards one of the beings this Will has created, to help him to overcome all that is fallible in him.

From a different viewpoint still, it is the impersonal rendering of a balance sheet to date. From another, the removal of a man's consciousness from kindergarten to grammar school or university.

Still another aspect is to look upon the judgement as a creation of the man himself. He has made his bed and now must lie upon it. The self now confronting him, as a result of all his life on earth, is essentially his own creation, one part of which comes home to him as a terrible stranger which it is now necessary for him to acknowledge and live with.

The judgement, and its pain, lies in reading the balance sheet and in acknowledging its truth.

All accounts agree that no exterior judge is met. (W. T. Stead's 'interviewer' is really his teacher, and not a judge.) In confronting and accepting the panorama the man is his own judge.

The most difficult problem for us in trying to understand the panorama process is how a completely objective presentation can come about of every event – physical, emotional, mental, spiritual – in one man's life. Who or what manipulates the panorama: a being? Or a mere recording apparatus? Or is it imprinted upon the innermost memory of the man himself, and somehow now reflected back to him, converted into the panorama or television scenes spoken of?

Some of the persons with whom he has had contact will still be on earth. How then is it possible for *their* side of interlocked experience to be accessible to *him* during the judgement? Again we encounter a process almost impossible for us to understand. Some accounts state that the memory or record of all events is implanted in some way upon the 'akasha', described as a subtle substance surrounding the earth – a gigantic representation or reflection of the lives of all its inhabitants. If all inner and outer events are thus imprinted upon an 'akashic' or 'etheric' surround (of which scientific discarnates have so far not succeeded in giving us any real description although some occultists claim to be able to perceive part of it) it would account for how it is possible, during the judgement, for a man to understand the thoughts and feelings of others, which he played a part in bringing about. At every turn we are confronted by our limitations in attempting to understand what is really meant by the panorama; discarnates nevertheless impress on us in their accounts that it has been their true experience. The profoundly mysterious event cannot be evaded – our private, personal past, including its mental and emotional events, however much we would prefer to forget some of them, lives on, in our personal present after death, and also in an objective present as some sort of record of events, as well as in its actual effects on other beings. This is a formidable reckoning.

Judgement, however, is not an absolute event but an episode, from which a future will grow with new developments. It is a jumping-off ground. How could it be final, in the sense of applying absolute moral standards which might be totally outside the previous or present comprehension of the person in whom the judgement takes place? It must be an interim thing relative to his sensibility. For serious and high-minded people who have taken a strenuous view of the moral nature of living, the judgement is likely to be more severe, not in the events depicted but in the impact on themselves, than it is in lesser persons. They will care more. Those of more ordinary capacity, who padded themselves somewhat from living in too testing a way, will at first not have so much capacity to care. A criminal would simply fail altogether to comprehend the standards by which a saint has lived his life. What the criminal would regard as the good life would fill the saint with abhorrence.

It would be distinctly naive, then, to look upon the judgement as a single, isolated event, followed after a period of purgation by an uninterrupted ascension into steadily more blissful areas of consciousness. This is an altogether too simple picture. Life and its aftermath make up something more complex and more grand. In the preceding chapter only four grades of character have been taken as examples: the criminals and wrongdoers; the self-deluding who go on pretending to themselves about human values, like 'Sir Rupert', and the Celtic brethren; the mediocre people who have taken an easy pathway on earth; and those who have lived, as Pauchard did, a strenuous inner life. Actually, of course, there are many grades, for every soul is different and countless adventures in living come about.

So the equipment of character a man brings to his reception of what the judgement shows him cannot really be separated from the judgement itself. Both set the stage for his growth into his own future. His own future *for what*? He is to encounter new experiences which will search out, just as life on earth did, his spiritual capacities; the life ahead will in its own way continue to be a testing ground. There are many capacities which he will still need to grow, and he himself will grow with them. He can only become a larger being by acquiring the necessary spiritual muscles. The more his future life offers him, the more he has to earn it at every step. He is, comparatively speaking, still a pygmy, and what the judgement has revealed to him is no more than a pygmy can understand.

Thus the early 'mansions' or 'staging posts' to be met with and described in discarnate accounts can be thought of as pictures of reality at which certain pilgrims choose to halt. These are very small pictures, carved out of a far larger spiritual landscape than is within the traveller's present compass, and which is, as yet, far too intense for him to bear. The ascent up the Jacob's ladder involves on each rung an ever-growing intensity of being. The purgations to be faced, for these are more than one are appropriate to the level of consciousness as yet gained.

The pilgrim has still to experience much which has so far largely been veiled from him.

CHAPTER 8

The First Heaven

1

The usual picture of life after death as a passage from one sphere to another, each more refined than the preceding one, assumes that the values of each sphere are worked through, learned and enjoyed as in a school class; and that then this particular classroom is left behind for good. This is another convenient simplification. It is more accurate to think of a process of passing through a number of layers of consciousness, and of man as not yet fully aware of himself as a many-levelled being, and who at these early stages is much less than his full self.

2

The traveller has next to enter what is sometimes called the First Heaven, and he has also to undergo a further purgation (described in Chapter 9). These are parallel and overlapping experiences, each as necessary as the other. In the First Heaven man lives through his true credit side, and in purgation his debit side. It appears that purgation does not need to be completed before the First Heaven begins; they are two opposite sides of the one coin. Probably in most cases the experiences mingle, the pilgrim choosing to move from one to another in turn.

On the credit side, he finds himself rejoicing in a fuller expression of all those things within him which are in resonance with his real nature, as opposed to the whims which he attached to his earth personality and which were reflected in his Summerland stay. Because this part of him is spiritually true, he finds it is in harmony also with his new spiritual environment. The two are on the same wavelength. He is gradually awakening more fully through a change of heart, to a consciousness which is within him and is also expressed in all around him, which is shared with many others, and where he can live and work in joy. Though it is truly his, it just as truly belongs to the ongoing life around him. In coming into his own, he finds his own is also the 'own' of others, a harmonious setting for continuation of his rightly attuned will to work, to grow, and to expand his vision.

The greater our advancement in spiritual development, the wider will become the circle of human beings to whom we can give our love. We do not love one being only in the world! Thus arises the wonderful harmony that then sounds as a perfectly sounding chord. Each note will chime by itself, but in harmony lies beauty.[1]

It is no static place of reward where he can sit back and take things comfortably; to believe so would completely belie the nature of what he is now attempting.

Though he does not at first fully understand all that is involved, the pilgrim now has the freedom to discover himself to be a much larger being than he has so far known. He begins this gradual rediscovery of and return to the whole of his own being. But only a small part of this will now be achieved in the First Heaven. Here is an account of one such rediscovery:

. . . There is . . . error in your conception of the *real* 'I'. You speak of it as being something separate from you and outside of you.

You will never reach it in that way.

The *superior* 'I' and the *inferior* 'I' – to use the expressions to which you are accustomed – *are one and the same reality.* Try to grasp this completely.

In fact, it is not the *superior 'I'* which must be 'reached', for it is always there – the very foundation of your life. Only your personal consciousness, which thinks of the *superior 'I'* like a dream, must *awaken from its slumber.*

Endeavour to identify yourself with *It*.

Perfect identification is realization.[2]

This has been described by another teacher as realising one's spiritual identity.

Such a process is best looked upon as a *transference* from one area of one's consciousness to a larger area. As this realisation takes place, the former consciousness will gradually melt away as irrelevant. This is an aspect of the putting away of childish things of which St Paul speaks. To a certain degree the traveller can move up and down within these layers of consciousness. As he progresses, more and more of his attention rests in his more refined levels. But a part of him may still belong to a lower level of himself which he has not yet shaken off.

So one must not assume that, once adjusted to the postmortem world, one has become all of a piece. A Glastonbury monk, hundreds of years after his death, speaks of this sort of division in his nature:

Why cling I to that which is not [i.e. the past of Glastonbury]? It is I, and it is not I, butt parts of me which dwelleth in the past, and is bound to that whych my carnal soul loved and called 'home' these many years. Yet I, Johannes, amm of many partes, and the better parte doeth other things – Laus, Laus, Deo! – only that parte which remembereth clingeth like memory to that which it seeth yet.[3]

3

The traveller is now placed in a world of intensified perception and of deepened emotional relationships. Having grown tired of the shallow pleasures which the Summerland offered, he now links with those who are dear to him in a more unselfish way, and rejoices in the other's nature for its own sake as much as for what it gives to him. The situation is, of course, a mutual one. Each finds joy in the nature of the other.

Graceful and beautiful landscapes are now pictured, filled with individual homes, with temples of worship and buildings which make up what can be best called a university of the spirit. This must not be written off as a fairy-tale, an imaginary picture which is no more than an emotional compensation for what has been lacking on earth. This First Heaven, too, is a mental creation, just as were the earlier regions of the Winter- and Summerland, but which exists for the fuller expression of the life of the soul. These beautiful landscapes and dwellings convey with them a sense of permanence, for most of what is learnt here will not later have to be unlearned. Much attention will now be given to study of spiritual laws and to exploring the inner side of subjects already known well and loved whilst on earth.

On the equally necessary outgoing side, one form of companionship is to give succour by touching the finer emotions of those upon the earth, either by a daylight telepathic influence or, perhaps more frequently, by direct or telepathic communication with them whilst they are sleeping. Such may be the source of some of the wise resolutions, the promptings of conscience, the increased insights which can arise within a human being and filter through to him on awakening from sleep or during his best moments of inner attention, but which of course his free will can accept or reject.

This kind of helpful influence can take a number of different forms. For instance there can be a fatherly watchfulness over a special talent, perhaps similar to that which the helper himself enjoyed when on earth.

John Remmers, an engineer who is a good witness, tells of his son's boyhood:

. . . Our home . . . was . . . adjacent to a large, well-kept farm where my son would daily play with the farmer's boy . . . Near this farm was a beautiful wood of various species of trees and wild plants. There, he would spend time alone. On returning home with specimens of plants he had gathered, he would proceed to explain to me [their characteristics and the] various parasites attacking them. I was astonished and asked one day how he had acquired this knowledge. His simple answer was, 'Well it just comes into my head.'

. . . One day he was sitting at a desk, drawing as we supposed, but instead he handed his mother a sheet of paper, requesting she read to him what he had written. He was not quite seven-and-a-half at the time . . . and just learning to read and write.

> 'I come to your home often. I lived in a cabin in the wood. I have changed my mind about some things. I am interested in this boy. In his later years he will be recognised as an authority in agriculture.   Thoreau'

Every word was properly spelled including the signature. We had never discussed Thoreau nor had any literature regarding this famed naturalist.

. . . Thoreau's prediction was fulfilled. Today Bert holds a very responsible position as a consultant in all branches of agriculture in California.[4]

Such help is kindly and beneficent, yet it can also have self-redemptive elements in it. Some report it as being a consequence of the judgement. It is interesting to speculate why Thoreau (if it were he) felt it was necessary to say he had changed his mind about some things.

W. T. Stead describes this aspect thus:

> We have then to spend time in close touch with earth, in order, by influence, to make good for our past misdoings; make good, as far as possible. Also we have the knowledge and full sight of the results of these earlier acts, and they do not bring happiness; but after that state is passed and we can bring all these things into proper perspective and form a table of work, which will gradually and continually be working out the results and troubles we have caused, then we can each one settle down to live here in freedom.[5]

Another type of help can take the form of general advice, useful to the listener's avocation, as when Sir William Barrett, F.R.S., speaks to his wife, who at the time was Dean of the London School of Medicine for Women.

You have an instinct very strongly for being alone at times. Not because you are bored with people, not because you're selfish, but some inner sense tells you it is necessary for your mental and physical welfare.

This is necessary to everybody, because the vibrations of another presence unless in perfect harmony are destructive and at times even dangerous to one's health. One wants to get away from noise, an instinct of self-preservation.

All human beings should be able to have peace and quiet, just as we expect to have fresh air, food, water and sleep, for the well-being of our physical health; but . . . we often forget that there are other conditions, excitement, noise, anxiety, and all the other more subtle and invisible elements which make up life – thought currents, electricity, waves of different kinds. We have ignored these through ignorance . . .

A time in each day should be set apart by everyone for complete relaxation – not only of body but mind, and immunisation from the destructive elements such as noise and movement . . .

Argument is the same; the clash of opinions, of wills, may be stimulating at times, but is destructive as a rule. In modern life there is so much that clashes, jars, fights, disintegrates.

I should say life is more destructive now in these strong though subtle ways than it has ever been, but the influence is ignored because the effect is not registered on the physical body, but through the nervous system.[6]

Two army generals, one now dead, one on earth, and close friends still, discuss their former experiments to try to produce communication with a machine instead of a medium. The one on earth was Brigadier-General Roy Firebrace, the name of the other (fully given by him during communication) is withheld from publication.

I am trying to grow closer – *grow* closer – *not* get closer – to the people with scientific and inventive minds over here, who tried to help us to create a machine. We still feel that the human element is the essential factor in true communication.

What could the S.P.R., and people like that put in place of this? There's something more than words – the same old subtle feeling of belonging.[7]

It is surely not to be expected too that musicians and other artists will after death lose interest in all that spoke so deeply to them, nor that they should not sometimes wish to help their fellow artists on earth.

Miss Jelly d'Arànyi, the violinist, was practising Bach's Sonata in E minor, using David's edition, which indicated an Allegro in the first movement. She was much surprised to get an unexpected advice to play

that prelude very slowly. Imagine or rather hear it with a lower octave; in fact hear it in octaves, then you will get that majestic sound Bach wishes for it, like a cathedral with immense width and the columns hammered out one by one. Space would become telescoped if speed is used. The whole of the prelude must sound heavy and supernatural.

This was followed by a discussion. . . .

Q. How should the tremolo be played?
A. Use only the left hand and keep to a low register.
Q. But that cannot be done.
A. Of course it can be done. If your left hand gets tired, you can use the right hand alternatively. The work is in the Bach–Gesellschaft.
Q. It is not so. I have carefully looked for it there and could not find it.
A. But where Vivaldi's themes are kept. This is what we remember and believe it to be correct.

J. d'A., though sceptical of finding the original work of Bach . . . informed an official at the Royal College of Music

. . . of her vain endeavours to find it. A new effort was made and she was brought a small volume of works by Bach, built on themes by 'Vivaldi', together with a work by V. The volume contained the sought for Sonata, exactly as the message had informed her . . . Bach had not put any mark as to the tempo in the first movement and the Allegro indication of David could not, therefore, be accepted as authentic. . . . The instruction contained in the messages was followed and the beauty of the work found to be greatly enhanced.[8]

Here the medium was her sister, Adila Fachiri, also a concert violinist, whose scripts pursue a number of themes, and not only musical ones.

Help is suggestive, rather than authoritative, as in the case of the communicator of Baron Palmstierna (the Baron was a Swedish Ambassador).

Do not accept everything we advise you as the only possible solution of matters in your lives. Remember that we judge differently than you on earth. Certain points we do not see as clearly as you because with us the big issues are in the foreground, whilst with you small things may spoil or help. We rely on your judgement and good sense particularly as we rarely see the bad points. You must not think that our views which are based on a spiritual existence are unfailing. Act through your own wisdom.[9]

4

The world of the First Heaven must be looked upon as still belonging to that area of experience which theosophists and occultists call *Kama Loka* or the astral world, the place of desires, where the soul, still conscious of unfulfilment as well as of fulfilment, works upon the inadequacies it discovered in itself through the judgement, and which it must overcome if it is to free itself.

On the other hand, insofar as it is concerned with a stretching of the self, the gaining of new insights, the listening to deep intuitions, and with gradually becoming aware of greater beings and greater areas of experience beyond itself, the soul may equally be said to be qualifying itself for entry into the mental world or *Devachan*, the world of the heavens, in which are found the beginnings of mental creation. Thus the areas which occultists separate out so sharply from one another are probably frequently experienced in the interwoven way already described, partly in freeing oneself from the past, partly in looking towards the future, so that early steps at the boundaries of *Devachan* are taken whilst much of the soul's work is still concerned in *Kama Loka* with its own past legacy of error to be made good.

5

At some time it will inevitably be asked whether any equivalent to sexual union exists after death. The idea may seem shocking to some; but might this reaction merely represent one's possibly peculiar notions of the supposed requirements of decorum in 'heaven'? It is clear that if a man really craves for the physical expression of sex it will no more be possible than to satisfy a craving for alcohol, for the very simple reason that he no longer has a physical body. Desires of a physical kind must go unsatisfied. But what if a desire is other than physical? Sex is a many-layered thing. Where a man or a woman has led a life without sex, deprived of it perhaps by religious prohibition, by a lack of adventure, through physical incapacity, or by the loss of a mate through war, the unfulfilled emotional desire can still be there. Take the account of T. E. Lawrence, of whose repressed and unhappy feelings towards women there is ample evidence in his earth life :

> I do not propose to detail all my hesitations and doubts nor my struggle with diffidence and life-long inhibitions. The monk and the prig in me were very strong . . . Much of my

reluctance . . . left me when M. explained the differences between sexual relationships here and those known on earth. To understand them it is necessary to remember that there has been a total change in the body substance and that the basis of all relationships here is purely emotional . . . Where an attraction between the sexes is felt, it is a pure emotion of love and the urge is to draw near and share the warmth and beauty one desires. Lust as such is hardly possible in this plane. If union takes place it is an interfusion of the two bodies and an ecstatic and satisfying experience far more lovely than anything one could experience in an earthly body. There is no question of the procreation of children so that all the more sordid side of the sexual relation is unnecessary . . . I found a girl who pleased me and who was gracious enough to approve of my company . . . We two have wandered happily in an enchanted land exploring the delights of an intimate companionship crowned by the magic of union . . . Without sorrow we both begin to feel the beginning of the inevitable withdrawal and we have discovered that neither of us had expected a permanent relationship. This has brought no disappointment but rather gratitude for a perfect experience shared . . . We are able to part with no regrets or anything but a great regard and affection for each other . . . So we have bidden each other farewell.[10]

Lawrence's experience surely has its beautiful as well as its pathetic side. As can be seen, it is rooted in a certain unreality; indeed, in carrying out the experience, both Lawrence and his partner found that each did not need the other's true self, but chiefly needed to overcome their own lacks and former withdrawals.

A communicator, speaking quite soon after death, has said: 'Men and women still have the same feelings towards one another as on earth, but without the biological urge.' How then are these feelings satisfied in persons more integrated than Lawrence? There are likely to be many levels, as our next witness says, where communing take a more subtle form. There seems some reluctance to tell us much about it, perhaps from the impossibility of speaking accurately.

. . . Mutual love in our regions . . . is so different from human sexual intercourse. . . . We feel our mutual love with varying degrees of intensity and the greatest degree is accompanied by a sort of temporary merging of one with another. It is done always in complete privacy . . . it is something very sacred and entirely lawful with a chosen partner who is of full affinity, and it leaves afterwards a sense of happiness which no words can express. Such unions are not meant to increase the population of Paradise, but are purely private expressions of love.[11]

Lawrence's experience was one of worth, but illusory in being projected falsely upon a partner with whom his relationship was limited. The experience just quoted differs since the relationship is a real one. It would be wise, however, to make room in one's imagination for later and deeper experiences between man and woman. This second experience is not the last word. Like all else in the First Heaven it is a fulfilment of earth consciousness, but only imperfectly aligned as yet to life in the Second and Third Heavens.

6

Descriptions of the First Heaven and of the Summerland can seem, on first reading, to be very much alike. Both talk of buildings, of a beautiful landscape, of the companionship of friends. The two states can easily be confused as we read of them. Yet the difference is a very significant one; it lies in the quality of life. Those in the First Heaven, as has been said, are aware of a more intense life around them, which permeates their consciousness and has both a sustaining and an evoking quality. An admirably simple description is given to the Revd Drayton Thomas by his sister, Etta :

'Form and colour in our world are identical with form and colour in yours. What I find so difficult to describe to you is, not what things look like, not the angle of a wall, the flowers, the trees, but it is THE FEELING.'

She repeated those two words very slowly and impressively, manifesting intense emotion while doing so. Then added, 'You yourself know, Drayton, there are times in your life when you have the feeling, which you can only describe as a sense of joy and uplift. But you cannot really describe it, can you? And it does not last long with you ever, but it is a taste of the feeling which we have all the time. . . . I cannot describe this feeling to you. It is a different feeling from that characterising earth.'[12]

Her father, the Revd J. Drayton Thomas, added a comment:

Remember how, sometimes unexpectedly, you are touched with sudden happiness, an extraordinary uplift, illumination and hope, and yet you are unable to tell others why. Really you are then sensing the hidden hope in life; that world which is hidden from you is revealed to you, the eye of the soul beholds that which the physical eye cannot see. Now, as we go on . . . we increasingly perceive the hidden beauty, love and hope in all things. It is not so hidden from us as it is from you. Etta and I are in a marvellous world.[13]

The 'landscape' is, as F. W. H. Myers wrote:

. . . in the state beyond illusion . . . you dwell in a world which is the original of the earth. Briefly, the earth is an ugly smudged copy of the world wherein dwells the subtle soul in its subtle body.[14]

Or, as W. T. Stead describes it:

You are now, whilst on earth, making your bodies for your next conditions. These are built up by your present lives and the quality of your thoughts. This world which I have been in a long time now, is the closest thing imaginable to your earth . . . You will say 'Oh, then it is only a reflection of our world'. It is not that way – the earth is only a reflection of *this* world. Earth is not the lasting world. It is the training school.[15]

7

Those in the First Heaven have now shed sufficient of the old heaviness of earth to be able to *utilise* the creative influences around them. They are learning all the while, and learning with a sure and certain hope; their life is one which is truly worth living; and when they find that the First Heaven holds for them purgative aspects also, they are able gradually to greet these too as creative parts of their new life, as necessary for their expansion as the joyful aspects. In a word, those in the First Heaven enjoy a widening of horizons which, except in briefest and most uplifted moments, is beyond anything they had been able to experience on earth. Furthermore, in spite of and beyond the purgative moments still to come at a deeper level than has yet been met, this joy is a continuing one; nothing can take it away from them, it cannot fade, because their soul has grown enough to *belong* now to these beginnings of creative life.

The outward sources of struggle, difficulty and limitation characteristic of life on earth have, of course, been removed in the earlier stages of post-mortem life – the management of one's animal body, the time spent in earning a living and maintaining oneself, the whole clogging effect of the life of clay, making for the dimming and drugging of the soul intelligence, the general effect of being confined as if within a diver's suit. Now in the First Heaven the soul is able to express its own nature more positively and freely because it is living in a world nearer to its own true identity. Instead of the deadening influence of earth, the soul is bathed in this spiritually stimulating atmosphere, with constant opportunity to respond to the whole activity of love which weaves itself around it, the sense of the unity of all life, the sense of living in a spiritual sunlight ever being poured out around one and into one's very being. This is the allegro side of life in the First Heaven. The travail and effort needed everywhere on earth are still required, but in a more refined mode.

The pioneer climbs the mountains of experience with much travail and effort. I might tell you this is not readily come by any more than it is in your world because it must of necessity be through application, through dedication and through experience that the true values of forward going can make themselves known and felt.[16]

As earth seasons bring growth and decay, so in the First Heaven spiritual forces which can be symbolically described as sunlight bring growth to the soul; and the element of decay is represented by those parts of its own character which the soul gradually finds it no longer has use for and which, as we shall see, it learns to cast away from it. The traveller will be called upon to face profound changes in his being. By our own dying day we certainly will not expect to have reached permanent solutions of the great earth riddles; nor, as we have seen, do such solutions come about in the early reaches of post-mortem experiences. The traveller is being prepared during this time for a further metamorphosis which will result in an acceleration in the growth of his stature, giving access to new levels of perception. A further discarding, this time of the post-mortem personality, lies ahead.

We will look at something of what this entails.

CHAPTER 9

The Second Death

1

We have spoken of the *allegro* side of life in the First Heaven. Now it is necessary to speak of its *penseroso* side. Man in the First Heaven still has the necessity to learn by sorrow as well as by joy, but the sorrow is of a soul quality, and the very reception of it is suffused with a deep sense of the growth it is simultaneously bringing with it. Unlike so much sorrow on earth, which strikes seemingly so harshly, unjustly, or in ways which cannot be understood, the sorrow in the First Heaven, whilst very real has a spiritual purpose which the soul understands and which, therefore, even whilst the suffering is being undergone, it finds consoling and uplifting.

The man who has reached the First Heaven feels himself to be still essentially the same man who was on earth and who has made his way through the judgement process. He has come through this with a sense of the continuity of his own personality. Now he has to get ready to shed altogether a large part of this familiar self. It is the price he needs to pay in order to understand deeper parts of himself beyond his present knowledge. He is like a man who has hitherto lived all his life in a familiar room, but who must now abandon that room and go outdoors where he will meet a larger landscape of himself.

How long the process of dying lasts! – I am still dying; I am divesting myself continuously of sheaths, and each time I perceive more and feel differently. . . .

My *true* life has begun now; the dream condition has ended.[1]

2

Most people do not find it difficult to accept the laying aside of their body at death. At the end of the normal life cycle it has so often become a source of trouble and difficulty; often, too, it expresses in its ills the gathering mental and emotional limitations accumulated during earth life and now forming an encrustation around the self. It is, however, a different matter to visualise this further process which the traveller must face, the yielding up and demise of the personal self, because it is becoming no longer tenable to live within its limitations. The traveller has to face that this personal self will in the end come to be as tedious as the physical body became, or would have become.

At first most of us fear casting off the personality we still regard as our true being. Yet really it forms so small a part of us. What is meant by the 'personal self'? It is the sum of all the pilgrim's memories of the experiences, thoughts and feelings which made up his sense of himself as a particular identity during his past life on earth, which continues to live on as the same familiar person after death.

Once the traveller ceases to identify himself with this aspect of himself, hitherto regarded as so valuable, and gradually sees it as really worth very little, he frees himself. Then he no longer fears to give up this self-imposed solitary confinement.

Strange that a human being often prefers to remain for long merely a part of himself, without knowing the rest, without knowing the freedom of yielding himself up to the God force, to which he really belongs. This is the nature of the experiences towards which his soul has now to proceed.

He can also be held up by things other than old personality quirks. Limitations are subtle and can reside within what one believes to be the very heart of one's virtues. Such limitations can take considerable energy of consciousness to overcome. Many persons hang pictures upon the walls of their room of the self, pictures of God and of the nature of the universe. Some find these pictures are very hard to give up. They often take the form of a religion to which one has given one's best allegiance on earth. The Catholic will still feel his eternal happiness depends upon his remaining a Catholic beyond death; and others will similarly hold fast to their own faiths. All faiths are indeed expressions of the good in man, of the soul life in him. For that very reason they can take longer to overcome than the more easily seen limitations of character.

The words of Father Tobe, who on earth had been a Roman Catholic priest, suggest the beginnings of a loosening from former dogmas, and the first infiltration of that sense of a universal unity which is strikingly present in so many discarnate statements. But in the main he is still bound up within his old Catholic terms.

> God is *known to us* in three ways. He is to us Creator and Father; he is to us Redeemer and Saviour; and he is our Indwelling Helper. You notice that I close almost every prayer in the name of 'the Father, the Son, and the Holy Ghost'. I believe in the Trinity, not as an absolute dogma, but as our human understanding of the unitary Triune God : Father, Son, and Holy Spirit. I never speak of this Trinity as if there were three centres of consciousness, or a Holy Father such as was crudely conceived by pagan tritheisms, for our only rational basis for religion is an ethical monotheism.[2]

Discarnate accounts speak frequently of groups, of coteries, of bands, of those drawn together in the First Heaven by a common link of religious affiliation on earth. They create a picture of what heaven is and mentally set it up around themselves. The existence of other similar groups and bands, each claiming certainties of their own, points clearly to the essential limitation of each. Part of their soul is living in a concept which is too small for reality; love and fear equally have brought them there. So old patterns of religious thinking can make barriers against progress, and the soul for a time may be well content to let it remain so. But with further living, religious ideals thus brought over and preserved are gradually discarded; people leave the spiritual area where they have sought personal safety. From separation they must move on to a more naked unity with all that lives, a brotherhood within the mysterious creative force which sustains all.

In order to make himself ready for this important step forward a price, as has been said, has to be paid, a yielding up of much which until now has been looked upon as part of the very self. The traveller withdraws deeply within himself in order to play his part in bringing about the new death awaiting him, the death of the personality. He casts himself upon waters of abnegation. Before the soul can pass on, says Myers,

> He must first shake off, cast from him any dogma, any special outlook which has shaped his mentality, which confines it, so that his vision is limited and his experiences are therefore also limited; consciousness of reality being thus withheld from him.[3]

Myers goes on to speak of the second death as 'the breaking of the image'.

The image which the traveller is casting off is his persona or 'mask', which is what the word 'personality' means. Now he has to find his *individuality* – that which is undivided from the spiritual realities which lie around him in a still somewhat hidden form. Hitherto action and enjoyment apparently unselfish have still been partly carried out for his own sake, or perhaps in order to obtain merit. The right hand, so to speak, is not always aware of what the left hand is really doing. To look for 'medals in heaven' is an illusion, for it implies the separative personality welcoming a reward for itself. All the good actions, kindly feelings and high-minded intentions he now enjoys can still retain something, if not necessarily a great deal, of a meretricious kind; they can be a jewel set in pinchbeck.

This meretricious element has to be eliminated. Even in otherwise satisfactory episodes of life lingering elements remain which need to be purged.

So this loosening process comes about, a gradual letting go, a slipping off of what has hitherto seemed oneself.

> Those who stand the tests . . . pass to another and altogether different and lighter land – and each becomes impersonal. Impersonal in the sense that they are no longer Jack Brown or Madge Black, they are now pure spirit people, and their former love, which had been a personal and individual thing, is no longer for one but equally for all. All are alike to all. The purest tissue of God Love binds one and all.[4]

It is easy to look on the second death and fear it as a sacrifice, and so of course it is. In facing up to the sacrifice before it is made, it is natural to cling with longing to the thing which has to be given up; indeed, that is why it has not been given up before. Yet it now proves to have been the very thing which held the person back. Sacrifice, after all, means to make holy, and holy means 'whole'. After the step has been made, one's nature becomes more permeable; it perceives and responds to a holiness now seen more clearly in all the life around one, and gradually becomes akin to it. Other beings, too, are able gradually to reveal to the new pupil more of their own nature, simply because he has now given himself the capacity to see and receive more.

> Of course, I have consciousness here, but it is not like so many on earth, a narrow self-consciousness. The old sinful self is lost and forgotten in a great humility, which is absorbed in the consciousness of God and of others, but one is not obsessed by self.[5]

3

It is a stupendous experience to cast off that personal self, for seen from the threshold it is largely a step in the dark. In the very casting off comes the transforming process, the *metanoia*, from which a new man is created. In Christian terms, it is the process of losing oneself in order to find oneself. So in the second death one withdraws the life from one's former local and now unwanted concept of oneself. What previously seemed so essential is seen to be no more than the chrysalis from which the butterfly will emerge. In the words of a discarnate teacher :

> Men will lose all the shells of unwanted matter accumulated around them . . . of a soul kind . . . and will become a spiritual and blessed company of brethren.[6]

Arthur Conan Doyle within three years of his leaving the earth – an unusually speedy time – sent this graphic account of the second death.

> . . . that Second Death, so marvellous and yet so terrible an experience. For in this life we cling with all our might to – Self . . . Why not, when it seems desirable to enrich that personality with all the treasure we can gather by labour of hand or brain. . . . We do not pass naked into the astral, but rather bear with us many an earthly treasure of knowledge, strength and pride of accomplishment.
> And then . . . crown and climax of all our striving, comes utter relinquishment – such is the marvel and miracle of the human soul and spirit.
> To relinquish knowledge, power, accomplishment, all that goes to make our personal self of claims and assertions; to relinquish self-pity, self-centredness, the hope of accomplishment for self; to bare oneself, to become nothing; to restore to the Giver of all . . . *all that one has and is.*[7]

It does not follow that everyone takes exactly the same route to the second death. As with other post-mortem events, people come upon experience in their own way and only when they are ready. It is surely characteristic that Conan Doyle, with his large-hearted forceful extroverted temperament, should embrace this experience with such courageous abandon. Other temperaments will not encompass it through one decisive and spectacular leap, but much more gradually. To them it may come as a smooth and steady loosening and lightening of their being. Their change of consciousness will steal upon them, as the dawn steals upon a new landscape. Many will be aware of considerable help from other beings who already live securely at these levels, who bring what can be looked upon as a downpouring of light, a grace from above, the outgoing expressing of themselves at a higher level in the hierarchy of consciousness.

The pilgrim is gradually helped to raise himself towards the same level. He is taken on a 'journey' which is really a journey of consciousness.

> One cannot rise much higher because one loses consciousness. Accompanied by someone of greater development, one can go farther afield; but, if one goes much higher than one's own awareness, a dreamy state comes on and nothing registers clearly. I was taken travelling in this way, so that I would understand it.
>
> One's awareness grows as one develops – quite naturally as a child becomes an adult in time. One grows mentally and spiritually.
>
> Time doesn't enter into this as it does in physical growth, of course. Some people here change rapidly and some hardly change at all. It is the *desire* to go forward that counts.[8]

Frances Banks, in describing her experience of changing consciousness, tells how the priest who had been her spiritual confessor often came to her after her death, conversing with her at her own level, but at other times – in her metaphorical description – she is enabled to visit him in his own spiritual 'home'. To do this she needs to be temporarily raised to his level. She finds she can support this state for only a short while. If she were to sustain it, she would become completely exhausted so she has to return to her own previously earned terrain. She tellingly describes this as a most curious sensation of 'dwindling back' into her everyday self. The larger self, which she became whilst in spiritual companionship with her old confessor, melts away and leaves her. Yet of course with every such experience she becomes able to sustain it longer, until she will gradually become able to achieve this state as her full consciousness, in the same way that her confessor already possesses it.

Following the second death, the pilgrim sees that this brings about a deeper capacity, alike for joy and for pain, as he faces and absorbs a deeper knowledge than hitherto of what his spiritual identity contains.

CHAPTER 10

The Second Heaven

1

The second death is the event through which access is gained to the Second Heaven and to the enhanced consciousness which this brings about. The transit is described thus:

> It is not separation . . . but . . . a feeling of complete serenity and peace, with no concern for anything, or awareness of people around you . . . you are supported by something that is almost unidentifiable, you have lost your own identity without any concern or anxiety about it . . . It is a true spiritual release, and for a little while you don't really know where you are . . . There is no feeling of distress. It is a kind of oblivion, but a conscious oblivion.
>
> Then you become aware . . . of what I can only describe as a harmonic reverberation around you, a beautiful ecstasy . . . You feel this divine, ecstatic, unified power with such indescribable joy that you just don't know what is happening to you . . .[1]

In F. W. H. Myers's account:

> . . . the soul enters into unconsciousness; and when he is born into the Fifth stage he has cast from him certain attributes that were his when he still inhabited the Image; for his soul was, in part, that Shape of Light he has now discarded.
>
> . . . there is this lapse into apparent oblivion, a stilling of all processes, a great calm . . . Here the soul seems to pause. Slowly, however, vision returns. . . .[2]

Max Heindel writes:

> . . . The change is made from the first heaven, which is in
> the Desire World, to the second heaven . . . Then the man
> leaves his desire body. He is perfectly conscious. He passes into
> a great stillness. For the time being everything seems to fade
> away. He cannot think. No faculty is alive, yet he knows that
> he *is*. He has a feeling of standing in 'The Great Forever';
> of standing utterly alone, yet unafraid; and his soul is filled
> with a wonderful peace . . . In occult science this is called
> 'The Great Silence'. Then comes the awakening. The spirit is
> now in its home-world – heaven.[3]

2

So far the pilgrim has learned to readjust himself to the experience of living on after death, to face the judgement, and to
abandon the personality in which he lived so closely on earth.
He is now ready to transfer his consciousness to his hitherto
largely unknown individuality.

He has become well aware that the journey he has been
taking has really proved to be a work of transmutation of his
former self. Gradually he has come to see the full effects of his
last earth life, and has cast from his mind and feelings the dross
in which he was then immersed. The fruit of that life lies in
the essence he has distilled out of his good deeds, and also from
such part of the dross as he slowly and faithfully transformed
into virtue. These were the fruits of his day's labour in the vineyard, and they have become part of his permanent self.

As he becomes attuned to his life in the Second Heaven, what
does he discover within his individuality? In the composite
picture of life after death, a further and highly important factor
now begins to emerge. It gradually comes to be seen that the
picture has a compelling logic pointing to reincarnation. In fact
accounts of life after death, when put together, do not really
make sense without it. For now the traveller discovers that his
recent earth life represents no more than the latest chapter in a

book, and that it is time for him to come to know the earlier chapters. Just as the essence of his recent life (as distinct from its details) has become imprinted upon his permanent memory, or *causal self* as it is more properly called, so in a similar way there is already imprinted upon his individuality the essence of many previous lives, which have all contributed to make him what he so far is. Perceptions and experiences await him, both joyous and the reverse, which will conclusively demonstrate that the pattern of reincarnation has already been woven deep into his life and will continue to be so woven. He moves into levels where a wider vision is permitted, and he is faced with a gradual return to memory of *all* these earth lives, of their results upon one another and upon his most recent life, and of the identity which he has borne through them all, the full history which preoccupation with his limited recent personal self largely hid from him. Frances Banks calls this process 'rejoining her soul'. He now comes face to face with the spiritual meaning of these events of his long past and with the task of gradually transforming the still remaining imperfections which he comes to see have over many lives continually distorted and dimmed his true spiritual shape.

There are times when we have to be set apart to undergo a retreat, in order to understand more of our development . . . During this retreat, I was shown not only my earth life, but the whole course of my evolution. . . . Once you have conquered and risen above the small self, you can go through the test . . . you can learn so much from it and yet feel no pain, because you see how each mistake was turned to your advantage in spite of yourself, by the light of the Divinity within you working as far as you would allow it to do so. . . .

You are able to see the line of gold which has persisted through everything, and you think only of that. You store in your aura all the lessons you think will be helpful to you in future intercourse with other people, or in any work that you may be given to do. . . .

I saw that through the whole course of my evolution, *comparison* was the attitude of mind which had led to my undoing again and again, or had weakened the good of the work I was able to do. I do ask you, never allow yourself to compare : never think to yourself, 'why was I given this and another given that, what was the difference?' If you could see, you would probably realise that there was no difference underneath the surface, it was simply a case of adjusting the gift to fit in with your evolution . . . the larger self knows the reality behind, it is only the small personal self, the mind, which makes you compare. . . .

I saw that often I could have developed several gifts which seemed to me easier to use and better suited to the work that I was doing, than the one I had developed; but the Divinity within . . . saw that it was for my good to develop a gift which might appear to me inferior. I even saw that sometimes, when I had developed a gift and was in danger of being proud of my success and taking too much to myself, the gift was veiled over . . .

It was interesting to see the same temptation being met round after round : and to see that if I had conquered in one round, the temptation was not put so directly in my way in the next round, or it took a more subtle form, and I therefore may have succumbed to it. If I did succumb, I found that in the following round that temptation assailed me on every side, and I had to right it almost to save my life, therefore I was forced to overcome it – a very drastic and effectual way of education. I saw that clearly, throughout my evolution, but I also saw that I was never faced with temptation in that very severe manner until I had come to a certain understanding of the Power that was in me and so knew that within me, I possessed the strength to overcome, if I chose . . . I could see how I have kept the same attitude of mind right through my evolution, beginning with comparison which always feeds the smaller self and usually strengthens self-will.[4]

There comes to the pilgrim also a blueprint of the new life he must undergo on earth. He studies the next part of the road along which he must travel. This blueprint will not, of course, be punitive, though it will include much that is regenerative in purpose : it will indicate a course fundamentally harmonious to his causal self, however difficult some forthcoming episodes are seen to be. He will very closely examine his equipment of character, and resolve how best to attempt to utilise the opportunities which will be presented to him.

3

Perhaps the most important change which has come over me in the period since I left the earth, is the deepening of the realisation and confirmation of the *serialised* life which we all lead. . . . There is a definite *continuing thread*. One meets old friends, tried companions, and former Teachers. From conversations and communions with them, and through listening to their stories, the missing portions of one's own experience return to memory, and the pattern is built up anew. Not that the pattern of the continued life was ever completely lost. As the chief actor in my own particular drama I had become, as it were, so immersed in the last act or chapter that the incidents, tragedies, lessons of the previous scenes had tended to grow misty. But now I am beginning slowly and laboriously to piece together these scenes into a whole, into a serialised effort at living. Many of the incidents which have been jogged back into my memory by the confrontation of its co-actors long obscured in my consciousness come as a shock to me. Could this have been how I thought, spoke, acted? What great similarity there is in all the acts, yet how different! The Essence is steady and serene; the persona changing and elusive. As I meditate upon some flash of memory, some bead on the chain of experiences either on this plane, the earth plane or some other plane, the Plan unfolds itself, only partially of course, to my fascinated gaze. Did I pass up this great chance? Did I respond in such a puerile way? Did I not learn to listen to those vague memory flashes that spoke to me from time to time during all the experiences which 'separatist' thinking often turned into escapades? Had I sunk so far into matter that I had forgotten lessons already learned, philosophies so often established, as Real to my mind?
Truly I must have. The comparisons fill me with dismay.[5]

A good deal of this review, as Frances Banks thus found, is chastening, saddening, and even tragic. It brings with it, however, a beautiful factor which offers very great consolation. For these events did not take place in spiritual isolation; in these past lives many significant episodes have been shared by other beings whom the pilgrim now discovers to be his intimate and long-term companions. Over many years and many lives he has shared travails and triumphs with them. In a deep sense they are his brothers and sisters, his companions of the spirit, and will always remain so. His task is no longer one for which he is solely responsible; as the horizons lift he sees that it is really part of a grander task, a group task shared between him and these others. This group, Myers says, can consist of a few, or of very many people. Their destiny is bound together in the fulfilment of the group task. The companionship and love within the group is very great.

As a result of this extended picture he is likely also to find that amongst the earth personalities he encountered in his most recent life one or two will now prove to be these true companions of old from the group. As he re-meets and more fully recognises these, he feels that he is moving towards his true spiritual home. He also comes to know that the word 'soul' has a wider meaning. The group as a whole is in a real sense itself a soul also, a group soul, and he is in very truth part of this soul. The bond, the common purpose, will not all be seen in a flash. This new and most important review which he is undertaking will be carried out gradually, until the various parts are gathered together and make a whole. He is also coming to know his part in the common task of the group. He has seen all his own achievements and failures. He can look forward to a highly purposive future. He can live in more and more of his own proper nature, have the joy of recognising it and the pain of knowing where he has denied it. This period of recognition of himself, his task and his companions will of course be accompanied by much action also in the world of consciousness around him. He could not have reached the beginnings of spiritual wholeness without having learned and many times practised the law of service, which declares that everything which is received must willingly be paid for by a corresponding act of outgoing service to someone who needs it.

The early stages of linking with a group are likely to be slow. Its members will not all be recognised as such immediately. Some may simply seem congenial and necessary associates in the performance of tasks of service which the pilgrim clearly sees he cannot carry out alone. If he is to help others who are struggling with the same problems and illusions which formerly troubled him, he finds he needs the greater wisdom and experience of his companions to refer to; for here he is still something of an apprentice. He will need it still more as he expands towards parts of himself which have until recently lain outside his reach. He needs their help in uncovering and bringing forth the ideal which lies in his own innermost self, for this is a guide to the reality for which he is searching and which will be also the keynote of the group.

'The imagination', wrote Keats, 'is like Adam's dream: he awoke and found it true.' The pilgrim is now experiencing such a revelation. He is like a man awakening gradually from an anaesthetic.

Pauchard describes his expansion as he first encountered his fuller self :

> First I saw Albert Pauchard . . . just as if he were outside of me . . . I realised that the '*I*' who was observing thus was not 'Albert Pauchard'.
>
> At that instant I gradually recognized *who* I was. I did not see this *real* 'I', but realized it by an inner warmth which kept on intensifying and increasing in light . . .
>
> It was as if from the bottom of my being *a vivifying light started to gush forth and glow in an ever widening sphere* ! . . .
>
> All this was accompanied by a feeling of inexpressible *joy, happiness and health* . . .
>
> I understood then that our 'personality' is only the 'shadow' of our 'I'. A 'shadow' which always moves towards perfection – through the lives on earth and the lives in heaven – and which forms itself according to the outline of the one who had given it existence. The outline of the real 'I'.[6]

This higher or causal self contains the sum of his experiences in incarnations on earth and beyond; and, as well, it includes the seeds, long ago planned and implanted within him, of tasks and fulfilments for the future. He still has an infinitely long way to travel.

As he begins to understand the inner essence of his recent life – as he can, now that he has loosened his grasp upon all its outer details – he comes to see how it was related to successes and failures in earlier lives on earth – his earlier 'days' of experience – and begins to take upon himself the burden of fuller knowledge of the pathway ahead. He sees that others in the group are dependent for the fulfilment of the common task of the group upon his efforts, as he is upon theirs. Success and failure occur individually, but their real meaning lies within a group context. As he looks, he will realise that often the pattern became entangled; in various ways members of the group whilst on earth have let one another down, hampered each others' purposes, just as at other times they have enriched, sustained and fortified one another. As all this unrolls before his eyes, his knowledge of himself expands into its fuller context. The destiny of the group is his destiny and he is enlarged by belonging to it.

He will become deeply concerned with re-establishing his many links, forged often painfully, sometimes with love, sometimes, for a short while, through apparent hatred, with members of his group. Yet the suffering brought about by these memories of failures in former lives also provides the spur which will enable him to overcome and eventually obliterate the scars they have left on his soul.

4

There is nothing exclusive in his relationships with those with whom he is thus intimately bound in spiritual companionship over the past and for the future; their essence is that men and women are spiritually related in an interior way to a number of other beings. Here is no possible room for jealousy. In finding one's group one has, therefore 'come home' in a much deeper sense than in the First Heaven. One has found one's vocation; one has found oneself. All the real concepts of discarnate living can only be understood in terms of growing unification, of a life that is less and less separative.

We do not know how far on into discarnate life men and women will still experience an intimate merging into one another, in however refined a form. As we have seen, this can be experienced at soul level, in part at least, in the later stages of the first heaven consciousness. Does the concept of the affinity, the twin soul, a concept dear to very many on earth, persist during and after rejoining the group soul, or is it by then discarded? Occult traditions state that the soul is really herma-phroditic, and that far back in time each soul split up into two parts, male and female, which will eventually again be reabsorbed into one another, at an equally far distant time in future. Certainly this strikes into the human heart with deep appeal.

When it looks for its twin soul, its missing, unrealised half, from another aspect the individual soul is really seeking its own causal self, the regaining of which places it beyond the hunger for the 'other', and giving it one kind of completeness within itself. Or the joy of the self contemplating the other – even if in heaven there is no marrying or giving in marriage – may be in some way a true reflection of God's joy in creating a universe which is other than Himself, and yet which is also Himself. The mystery will solve itself in the end. Meanwhile it has to be enough to say only that in some form men and women will continue after death to share their delight in one another as long as this is appropriate to the changing levels of consciousness at which they are functioning.

5

With the expansion of consciousness, there comes a change of outer form. Gradually this becomes less fixed and more flexible; the pilgrim's etheric bodily outline no longer has the necessity to identify itself with a set outer form. By losing its firmness of outline, it comes to be able to radiate and express more readily all the varied responsive and inward parts of its nature which now make up the texture of the pilgrim's life. The man becomes, as it were, clothed with himself, expressing perfectly every quality which he has truly made his own. His aura is now his 'surround', a pulsating changing shape of many colours, expressing far more perfectly than could any fixed bodily shape his living relationships with all the beings he meets, together with his feelings of awe and worship, which are his deep response to the beauty and truth of the universe around him. In this aura delicate and vivid shades of colouring can be detected, growing and diminishing in response to all that it meets, the face remaining as the main organ of expression of the beautiful individuality within. This is the outer, slowly growing transformation which responds to the growth and refining of the inner nature.

> Here everyone is clothed in their own light and it would be impossible to copy your fellow spirit as his garment is the outcome of his soul. No earthly garment can have the variety of each spirit . . . as their colours which are their clothes, scintillate . . . according to the development of . . . [their] feelings.[7]

At a later stage, as beings advance further still, deepening, widening and losing themselves in the greatness of the whole, they appear more as a presence than a shape, communicating by thought and feeling which translates itself instantly and accurately to its recipient. But this presence can still be condensed temporarily into a shape like its former self when this is appropriate in order to confront those at levels lower than its own.

This attempt to describe the indescribable may at least throw a little light upon the nature of certain encounters which are now likely to face the pilgrim.

Associated with this period of the gradual transfer of awareness away from the personal to the larger self are certain peak experiences which arise from an encounter with an advanced being. This of itself can bring an immediate expansion of horizon. It will come at a time when it will best bring an acceleration and illumination, imparting an energy for taking further steps forward.

Pauchard describes two such peak encounters, the first more immediately personal, the second deeper and more impersonal.

> . . . I instinctively raised my eyes – and there they met and gazed into the most radiant eyes one can imagine! A beautiful smile, so infinitely good, revived my whole being. . . .
>
> Those were the eyes of one who represents for each one of us, the Heavenly *Father*. . . .
>
> The Heavenly *Father* appears whenever the moment comes – to every one of us – under the form of *our own highest ideal.*
>
> With many people this form is that of Christ, as He has generally been represented by the artists. . . .[8]

Many accounts describe a meeting with the Christ, some of them at very early stages in discarnate life. Most orthodox Christians before their death expect and long for such a meeting. With no wish at all to offend or hurt those with deeply held and cherished beliefs, it has to be stated that realistic appraisal points to an incorrect identification in many of these Christ-figure encounters. It could very easily arise that a close guide or teacher is, from his brightness, taken to be Jesus. It need be no more than His messenger, or a being, as Pauchard says, who is seen in the form which represents the viewer's own highest ideal. The meeting may be with the one who is the head of the spiritual group with which the viewer is linked in his essential nature. Does it really matter if the longed-for meeting is postponed? After all, there is an infinitude ahead in which it can eventually take place.

Whatever may be the situation, or situations, in this delicate matter, there can be no offence in suggesting, however deeply sincere the narrator, that more than one explanation is possible. Perhaps this sheds light, for instance, on how Sally, Rosamund Lehmann's daughter, experienced her encounter with her ideal figure :

When I stood in the conscious presence of Christ, I felt . . .
as though I had been painlessly put through the mincer and
reconstituted a better and a saner Sally. Everything Christ
touched is so *sensible* . . . The ecstasy and the thrill and the
joy of His presence were there of course; but to balance it all
was a deeply *practical* ray of sensibility.[9]

Pauchard's second peak experience was his meeting, along
with a company of others, with one whom he calls an *Awakener* :

I met the *Great Old Man* . . .
   When we are before Him, it feels as though the flower of
our soul expands under the rays of sunshine . . . each one feels
the warmth of His presence penetrate to the innermost fibres
of his being. A light is born within us. . . .
   He does not act – *He is* ! He seems to be absorbed in Himself and not to see anything nor anybody. And yet – strange
contradiction – *each one feels* a direct contact with Him –
and His sole presence makes the seeds of wisdom, love and
kindness which lay in the heart of everybody grow and develop
by themselves, just as the seeds in the ground under the first
warm sunshine in spring.
   The beauty and greatness of this Figure are beyond description. He . . . gives the impression of being a Rock and a Sun
at the same time : the impression of something unshakeable
and eternal.
   *It is a vision which lasts only a moment, but of a lasting
effect.* After that one is no longer the same. It is as though
from a child one has grown into maturity.[10]

Frances Banks's experience came whilst she was reviewing her
former incarnations :

I have had the wonderful illumination of being transported
by thought, temporarily to . . . where I was in contact with a
great Soul . . . one of the Divine Company . . . I understood
in silence all that He was communicating to me. It was as if
my journeys were unrolled before me . . . I was . . . at times
joyful, sad, proud and ashamed. Yet He never uttered a word

of blame . . . 'I am, I was, I always shall be' I recall thinking. As if in answer I saw Him – in flashes – as He was when I had contacted Him in my various states of Being, for he had played a part in many experiences and always as the Brother, the Mentor, the Inspirer. 'And I knew Him not' I thought with sadness. 'I remembered Him not.' As I looked His Face was the Face of infinite limitless Love. In my inner 'ear' sounded . . . 'Neither do I condemn thee.' . . . I was suffused with new joy, great hope and a deep strength of consciousness. I was so moved that I found myself weeping inwardly.[11]

Such deep and significant experiences are milestones in individual spiritual progress. Afterwards the pilgrim cannot be the same; he has grown and deepened, and has come to recognise that in his being he is essentially undivided from those who are his peers, and from the stream of spiritual light from higher beings by whom he is supported.

Can everyone, then, expect such an encounter after their earth life? Perhaps not necessarily. Because they are peak experiences they can only come about when the soul is ripe to receive them. Some may not reach this ripeness between one incarnation and the next, and will first return to earth again for further cleansing. Then, after this cleansing, they will inevitably gravitate to such an experience. Meanwhile, it has not been foregone or denied to them, but only postponed. It is waiting for them.

The further we attempt by inward speculation to understand a little of the deeper worlds beyond death, the harder it becomes to keep one's bearings. Once again it must be said that the danger is always to create divisions and distinctions which represent little more than conceptualising limitations. Spiritual growth, like the growth of nature, comes about in its own rhythm, and former limitations melt away as a man finds himself growing into larger concepts of being. He enlarges himself as life enlarges itself around him.

When one is speaking of the First, Second and Third Heavens, of earlier and later purgations, or of the group soul, it still remains very hard to avoid analysing life after death as if it were a matter of different realms. One is giving names to aspects of consciousness as if they were separate areas of living and ignoring the inward links by which, so to speak, they pass into and through one another, and which any man finds as soon as he is able to expand his being sufficiently. Present discarnate teachers prefer to speak less of spheres and regions, and more in terms of a merging, a deepening of consciousness, a process of organic, if many-faceted, growth.

Whether he is on earth, or in the Summerland, or in the heavens, and whether he is aware or quite unaware of it, every man is held within the consciousness of other beings who are concerned with his spiritual awareness, and with whom he shares just as much, or as little, as his own growth of being allows. Loving spiritual concern flows through the cohorts of mankind as blood flows through and nourishes the whole body of a single man. He already belongs to all that is around and beyond him to which his eyes are closed until he himself is ready to open them.

Therefore, these areas or kingdoms which, due to limitations and inconsistencies of words and thoughts have to be described separately, really form a single pattern within existence, a seamless garment of unfolding human awareness.

CHAPTER 11

The Group Soul

1

In trying to visualise life after the second death when men and women live increasingly as part of a group soul, one can still often be trapped into thinking in terms of a personal path in the soul life, thinking back to concepts which the traveller will really have discarded. Instead of a personal path, he is learning to think in terms of making, within membership of the group, an infinitely small contribution in the total process of the forward-going of mankind. The qualities needed to qualify, not for admission to one's group, since one is already essentially within it, but for recognition of and conscious participation in its work, involve a high degree of negation of self and self-interest. Without question these qualities form one page in the necessary passport. Only at such a level does the fullest mutual spiritual support become possible between group members, as distinct from quite different, dear and intimate, but personal companionship.

. . . I meet my fellow workers . . . We decide eventually on a plan of action, just as you would on earth. Sometimes we feel there is some direction or advice that is necessary in order that we should know the best way to proceed; in that case we open our minds; in other words, we all by agreement remain silent and receptive . . . now I find myself able to open myself with ease to inspiration . . . The message comes – we all respond to it – we are gathered together with one mind, one idea . . . when the call comes it does not come in the form of a voice or bell ringing. It is a mental call. One, or two, or three, or four may hear it first, before the others, according to the degree of their receptivity. We rise collectively, and those of us who have visited the higher planes before reach out to any persons who have not done so, just as you might hold out your hand in order to aid strangers along a difficult path or staircase to which they were not accustomed.

There is no feeling of danger or strangeness in it at all – none whatever; but we find ourselves ascending, the feeling is ascending . . . Myers said to me it was a reaching *out*, a travelling *out* rather than up . . . As one travels out, one becomes aware of the different atmosphere. That I cannot quite explain to you. It is an atmosphere in which the details of one's surroundings do not seem so important. . . . And one is aware of the *oneness* of things – the infinite; as one travels away from the planes of finite life, finite ambitions, finite imagination, one becomes more conscious of the infinite love, infinite power and understanding, and above all, one becomes absolutely conscious that everything is working towards the ultimate good of everybody.[1]

An essential factor lies in recognising that in giving oneself up to this mutuality one becomes more, not less than before. Conscious membership of the group soul leads to enlargement of being, and this membership must be conceived as part of the very meaning of oneself. As one discarnate teacher put it to a group he had drawn together on earth : 'I am part of yourself; being with me will be an exquisite satisfaction.'[2]

Over and over again it appears in various pictures of post-mortem life that spiritual knowledge is not an abstract thing primarily learned from a book or taught therefrom, but springs from a quality of recognition through transmission and participation from one person to another. Such transmission is not by preaching, still less by interference, but simply by being one's own aspect of truth, which then radiates itself to others. A group is likely to be the recipient, custodian and means of expression of a truth of which each member holds, and is able to express, a facet, and which will finally only be held fully and completely by the group when functioning as a whole with its spiritual leader, the inspiring force behind it. Thus the total being of a group soul will express a spiritual truth which is rayed out in many directions by members of the group, as a diamond flashes its facets on all sides.

Each group is unique and yet in harmony with other groups, though doubtless differing in the tone-colour of its intention and purpose. In this way the symbol of the diamond can be enlarged further, for each single facet would now represent a complete group soul in itself.

2

Whatever can be written necessarily smacks of limitation. A group will have a particular spiritual contribution which, with the help of all its members and over a considerable period of time, it will plant upon earth and help to establish there.

The further one goes out or up, the more . . . one draws near or nearer to the infinite source of all good. We reach what might be called another shore – yes, I will call it that – it always appears to me as being another shore. As we reach it we are conscious of the approach of other beings who hasten to welcome us. They know we have heard their call. A curious feeling comes to us as they approach us, a feeling of added power, sharpened intelligence, greater hope, greater courage comes to us like the first touch of an exhilarating wind that blows suddenly from a new quarter. Whoever these people may be does not matter at the moment, but they are those who have passed through one sphere and then another during many centuries of time as you know it. They are the teachers, the philosophers, the saints of the past. Their names are not bandied about as the names of famous people on earth; one simply feels, 'This is a great man, he brings with him power, a great knowledge.' . . .

We are shown the harmony and the beauty of this higher plane, something we are not ready for yet, but which gives us greater promise of joy to come, which we can take back with us to our own plane, and which spurs us on to further preparations for ourselves and for you.[3]

Thus, the group soul of which Myers is a part may have, as one of its tasks, that of establishing in minds upon earth the idea of the group soul itself, so that it gradually becomes a part of the creative understanding of many people.

One of the complexities which tax us is how far and in what way the individual members of a group are related to its central spirit or leader. Myers, if his idea has filtered down to us correctly through his sensitive, implies that all within the group are 'contained' within the one spirit.

Myers goes on to refer to the group as 'This brotherhood within the one being'. Again this implies that all a man's struggle towards perfection is not for himself. Immensely it gains strength from being carried out on behalf of the unity which is within the group, and is the group. Here a new, rather strange factor enters in; that the experience, the fruitage of the lives of other members of the group is, in a mode hard to understand, available to him also; not just in terms of shared companionship, but to be absorbed and utilised as if it were his very own experience.

At first sight it might seem unfair to be able to claim the spiritual advantage of experiences which someone else has carried out. But is this really a concealed selfishness, based on a sense of possession? Possession is the very thing that is subdued within the group relationship. After all, at everyday level, we feel no scruple in using the roads and walls, fields and buildings created by the sweat of our forebears. In the group it could be irrelevant which members have won certain experiences. Once absorbed, they belong to the group as a whole. Thus there could be an overlapping and interblending, a sharing of the essence of various experiences.

Rosamond Lehmann, after the tragic early death of a daughter with whom she felt the closest of affiliations, wrote of the :

. . . Extraordinary merging of myself and herself which occurred quite independently of my volition directly after her death. I have never been able to describe it and can't now, except that I felt a large invisible Plus had been added to me! – invisible, intangible, but absolutely solid . . . I saw from then on how incomplete I had felt before she was born.

Readers of *Candles in the Sun* will remember that what can best be called an access appeared to reach Krishnamurti shortly after the death in early manhood of a brother to whom he had felt a very close attachment. It is as if he now discovered within himself a larger state of being of which his brother formed a part. One speculates that earth experiences such as these, felt as a great and enriching privilege, foreshadow only to a limited degree the fullness which communicators tell us will be discovered later by all within a group.

Selfhood dies hard. Group relationships at first sound all very well, with the other members of the group draped conveniently around oneself. It is, of course, not like this at all. The self comes to recognise that it is less itself when alone, and more itself – only really and truly itself – when it is operating as part of this team. The minds and feelings of other members of the group are open to one another through telepathic intermingling. Although each retains the right to his own privacy, there is little doubt that the sharing becomes more important than the privacy. Frances Banks, in speaking of 'coming home' to her group, recognised that when separated from it or straying from it, she had been a lesser self. Hers had been the heartache which caused the prodigal in her to return. Love for members of the group widens into an impersonal love, though no doubt limiting elements will remain for a long while.

Because we live in communities do not imagine that we have alien feelings for those who live in others. We are all working for one and the same Master. The whole system . . . is so different for those who believe in the Great One's absolute purity.

You can be alone here, but, curiously enough for you on

earth, after you arrive . . . you do not wish to be alone and that desire completely vanishes after a period. Here there is no hiding . . . thoughts are open to all.[4]

A group moves slowly forward as the individuals within it discover their own true identity. Myers says that a group will not move beyond a certain point until every member of it has in the fullest sense rejoined the group, and achieved his own particular role in it. It would indeed be difficult to conceive of part of a group as having passed beyond contact with others who belong to it. Such an idea is an offence against the whole idea of spiritual unity. Whilst a group soul is incomplete, still struggling towards its own purpose, even the highest members of it are likely, to some extent, to be enmeshed within this task and thus to suffer under its limitations. By their very care for those temporarily incarcerated, they submit to a linking thread of limitation within themselves. This is their willing sacrifice – not to go so far forward as to become unable still to link with those on the lower rungs within the group.

The spiritual leader of the group is best conceived of as a great being, living within depths of spiritual reality quite beyond the present reach of the members of the group. This great being, in turn, will have received the basic archetypal plans for the group from higher levels still. It will be his task to interpret these in terms which those who belong with him will at present be able to take into themselves. Between any member of the group and its great central leader, the relationship is well expressed as one of spiritual fatherhood and sonship. There will also be intermediaries, themselves members of the group, to whom will be delegated something of this relationship. The pilgrim will find one who also in a fatherly way is nearer to him than the leader, one whom he will come to accept and trust in freely given love, who shows unmistakably that he holds the keys needed to unlock his nature and bring to it expansion of being. Discarnate teachers describe an interfusion and interblending of such a kind that the present barriers between individuals lose something of their meaning. One teacher says :

I am not a person, I am but a reflection of your better self.
I am part of a consciousness . . . That consciousness you aspire
to at the moment is part of yourself.[5]

Another, speaking of a gathering of people at soul level, says :

As we look deeper we see that these souls are all linked to
you. On the very closest plane, the astral plane, these souls
are attached to you as guides and helpers; they seem to be
part of you, so close are they to your soul. Then we look again
and see that these guides are even more . . . They are aspects
of your own soul, parts of your own soul . . . they are all
attached to you and are part of you. Can you understand
this? So as you expand your consciousness . . . you become
many brothers.[6]

3

Can the group leader become known to those of the group on
earth? One group has been described in various scripts as having
its spiritual source in Francis of Assisi. The saint is held to be
speaking to one on earth who is a member of his group :

Ye have partaken, ye are part of me, thy spirit is part of
mine. As the son to the father, so are ye to me . . . Lorenzo
[another member of the group] is as another and perhaps
lesser father to ye. A fold of Francesco is he, and ye are
another fold. For the spirit holdeth within itself other spirits,
and ye are within Leonardo as ye are within Francesco, but
nearer Francesco than Lorenzo are ye . . . Ye are the child
of my spirit and have been nigh unto me from the Beginning
and in no wise can ye be loosed from the spiritual link, for
ye are as a blossom on my tree and can bloom on no other,
for through me do ye derive from the Great Father of all
and from that which is Francesco have ye been brought
forth.[7]

It has been said before that unity within a group in no way
involves exclusiveness towards those outside it. Exclusiveness

would be utterly foreign at this level of awareness. A figure like St Francis must surely be regarded as flowing out in love to the whole world, as looking outward far beyond those in his own group.

It is possible also that a leader of a group will wish to make himself available at many levels of consciousness, as indeed St Francis seems to do. A former Doctor of Divinity thus describes his meeting after death with St Francis:

> In his mind is no personal desire that some one person in whom he is interested on earth should progress or help humanity more than another. He wants every person who is capable and willing to help. He wants to uplift life on earth mentally, spiritually, and he will do it for anyone whom it is possible to work through. . . . To my utter surprise, St Francis greeted me as a friend, as someone whom he knew personally and recognised. This was overwhelming to me.
>
> I thought I knew him, but I did not think he knew me; he seemed to know me well, and impossible as it sounds, he seems to have followed my work in certain directions with personal interest, if I may use that word in the face of what I have just said. He took my hand and I was conscious of the most extraordinary warmth of feeling, affection, friendliness, sympathy, understanding that I have ever felt. . . . [It] seemed . . . as if I were basking in the very spirit of comradeship . . . He told me I should be given work on the earth that would eventually clear the way so that love and mercy could find and take their rightful place in life on the earth as they do in the higher spiritual planes. But he also explained that there is so much clearing up to be done first. That the spirit of elimination would be used first, and that it might be a very painful process, as the process of spiritual elimination always is.[8]

On one occasion it seems that the saint for a moment even stood very close to one on earth who was a member of his group. Laurence Temple was an architect and a church he had designed in honour of the saint had been consecrated, but because of the architect's anger over unsuitable colours provided for the furnishings which spoiled his design the consecration service was not worthy. So on a later date he and a few friends gathered in the church for what was to be an unannounced reconsecration. Temple describes what he himself then saw :

> There was Presence in the church. We were all agreed afterwards about the moment. For me . . . quite vitally, the great Brother was in the aisle by my left shoulder.
>
> At this moment he was not merely the little friend of the birds. Once or twice recently he had appeared to . . . others, and he had come as a very great Being. In that manner he stood in the church, and the radiance from him streamed far beyond its roof and walls. In that same moment I seemed to know that about him were great angels; great of stature and of profound beauty.[9]

Later, he asked Mrs Hester Dowden about this, and this reply came from the so-called 'Francesco' of her script :

> Yea, ye were lifted out of the body for a moment, and as a child is lifted, that he may see over a wall that is too high for him, so were ye lifted and saw for a few moments that which is too high for ye.[10]

Within the group, then, levels of ascending consciousness are cradled by and derived from deeply spiritual beings; thoughts are implanted within members of this group as acts of creation to be passed down for the ultimate benefit of the earth world. It is the principle of relay at work.

After her death, Mrs Willett, the outstanding automatist of the S.P.R. cross-correspondences, described a mystical experience she had whilst on earth :

> I recall one occasion uniquely intense . . . It seemed as if, lifted up on wings, I was in a state in which I understood all things. All were summed up in one and brought to a point. Bliss in such union was mine.[11]

She now came to realise that this experience resulted from Frederick Myers's mind flowing into hers from beyond, and that he was a member of her group soul. The experience was union with the spirit of her group and Myers the agent who brought it about. It was less a piece of direct and private insight, and more of a shared participating experience. Mrs Willett goes on to say :

> The human being's soul belongs to, or is derived from a Group Soul, which is inspired by one spirit. If we make progress in the after-death, we become more and more aware of this Group Soul. It is more than a brotherhood, it is organic, an organized psychic or spiritual structure. Its spirit is the bond that holds together a number of souls. The spirit might be described as a thought of God, or the Light from Above – the Creative Light from Above. It has an apartness from God, as is the created thing from the One who gave it life. At first an embryo innocent, it has to gather a harvest. . . .
> A number of human beings who have mystical experiences assert that in those ecstatic moments, they have obtained union with, or absorption into, Deity. Actually it has been usually union with the spirit of their Group Soul . . .[12]

Mystical experience, sometimes at least, thus seems to spring from the level of an intermediary being.

It has sometimes been said that this world of earth is a thought in the mind of God and that if God ceased to think it then the earth would disintegrate instantly. This is undoubtedly in accord with the general tenour of discarnate teaching, presenting a picture of spiritual activity at a thousand different levels, whereby parts or fragments of this thought of God are held, rejoiced in, and then relayed down in forms which are steadily more concretised, dense and, as it were, wrapped round with layers of earth, as they descend to those still on earth. As the occult saying has it, 'As above, so below'. Man in his best insights is only repeating perceptions already familiar to those in the spiritual world and passed directly down to him.

In the next chapter, we shall see the pilgrim approaching the furthest experiences yet possible to him, and how these offer him the opportunity for utilising them in very important ways for his own future.

CHAPTER 12

The Third Heaven

1

Survival of death is not, of course, to be equated with immortality. Many churchmen today prefer to play down the idea of personal survival and look instead to a concept of eternal life. This brings us to mysteries of being very hard to understand.

We have seen that when Frances Banks spoke of 'rejoining her soul' the process included the gradual recollection of the essence of each of her past incarnations. In these regathered seed kernels were retained the fruit of all her various attempts to realise her true nature and express it both on earth and between her earth lives. Quaffing her deep draught of memories, she saw that the essences of all these lives are linked, like the beads of a necklace upon its chain; each is different though related to the whole pattern. The soul looks before and after. As a teacher has put it :

> The higher etheric or soul body is a creation not of physical birth and not of eternity, perhaps, but of long ages past. In this soul body we find woven the experiences of the past, the higher worlds, the higher planes of being.[1]

It would deny the root meaning of the term to say that this is immortality; but it is certainly life continued over a very long span. Nor does it exclude the possibility of either immortality or of eternal life in some still more inward, more essential part of the self. In terms of the soul, as distinct from the spirit, the experience recorded in these life memories lies, after all, in the realm of imperfection. The soul is transforming itself over an immensely long period of time.

If churchmen throw away the concepts of immediate survival of death, and then of immortality, in favour only of eternal life, this surely is to require too much too soon. It is also to deny the value found in the intermediate parts of the journey. Let man be content first with survival of the personality, then with recognition of his long span of experiences, past and to come, and only later, within the higher self, lose himself in eternal life, when he has sufficiently perfected himself. Teachers tell us that this takes a very long time indeed.

2

Man, as we have seen, has been learning to give himself up, aspect by aspect; first his body, which often in repeated earth lives he is glad enough to shed; and then all those personality aspects which he has brought into being in these incarnations, preserving only the essence of their experience, which he has woven into his individuality. All that he sheds, he sheds because his true being has no need of it. But for a long time over many lives man often still clings to parts of himself which have limited value, thereby denying his true path to eternal life.

Severe and painful in some aspects though it may be, discarnate life is nevertheless merciful, for the soul is allowed to proceed at its own pace. In the mental world of the Third Heaven, a vision of perfection is just as difficult for the traveller to accept, though for opposite reasons, as is the purgative picture of his past errors. It is too grand for him to encompass fully. As T. S. Eliot says, humankind cannot bear very much reality. Only very gradually can the soul assimilate itself to the heavens around it.

Available accounts of the Second and Third Heavens are brief, due to the difficulty of conveying the quality of life there in terms which we can understand. These heavens primarily belong to inward levels of being. This is why they are part of the mental or spirit world. They are worlds of perception and of creative planning.

In terms of consciousness the Third Heaven is to be regarded as a very extended area, with a far greater difference between the Third and the Second Heaven than there is between the Summerland and the First Heaven, or between the First and the Second Heaven. Hence many lives of fresh endeavour on earth are likely to be needed to enable the pilgrim gradually to earn the right to a true place in the Third Heaven. Simpler souls, still on the earlier rungs of the ladder, it is declared, need to reincarnate sooner, coming back from the First Heaven without entering those beyond, because it is directly from earth that they can best learn the lessons next needed.

The pilgrim who has reached the Second Heaven and become aware there of the obstacles which over many lives he has placed in his path will now in the Third Heaven receive further perceptions into his true potentialities. Thus in these two heavens he finds himself standing in a particularly intimate way between his own past and his future. A sojourn in the Third Heaven is strictly limited by the degree to which a man can reach and attune himself to those around him. Most will not be able to absorb more than a fraction of the living wisdom which is being poured around them from the pulsating thoughts of the beings they will encounter there.

So an important distinction has to be made between those who are true denizens of the Third Heaven and are capable of fully expressing in their own nature its activities, and those others who only touch its fringe, entering briefly into it in order to absorb such instruction as they can understand and bear before the inexorable necessity arises to return again to earth.

The posthumous Myers, in speaking of those who belong to the Third Heaven, clearly regards them as high in the human hierarchy. Indeed, he goes so far as to describe them as 'Lords of Life'.

. . . on this level of consciousness pure reason reigns supreme. Emotion and passion, as known to man, are absent. . . . Such equanimity becomes the possession of the souls [in] this last rich kingdom of experience . . . they are capable of living now without form, of existing as white light, as the pure thought of their Creator.[2]

It is probable that some who make their home in the Third Heaven no longer have the need to reincarnate on earth, but work extensively from there to help humanity forward. The profound beings described in Chapter 9 (see pp. 141–2) – Pauchard's 'Great Old man' or Frances Banks's 'One of the Divine Company' – almost certainly belong to the Third Heaven. From time to time such beings assume an appearance, an image of themselves, in order to reach down to the souls of those in their care who are still working at lower levels. Here they help to bring about a re-creation within the beings of these in the way Pauchard tried to describe. This is why he called the Great Old Man an 'Awakener'.

In this part of our field it is again particularly important not to be too schematic, not to attempt to define closely the boundaries between what belongs to the Second and what to the Third Heaven. If Frances Banks, as her story strongly suggests, was labouring upon herself in the Second Heaven, then when she came under the influence of the one who belonged to the Divine Company she momentarily reached up and found herself living within part of his consciousness in the Third Heaven; and in touching this vision of herself she was also touching momentarily a fragment of her own potential third-heavenly self.

It has been said that in the Second Heaven the pilgrim receives what can be called a blueprint of his next life on earth. Who, or what, then, produces this 'blueprint'? The pilgrim himself needs, of course, to understand and work upon the blueprint; it appears, however, that it is primarily planned and created in the Third Heaven by these greater ones who can see his essential truth of being in a way that he cannot yet do out of his own resources. They transfer to him this vision of his potential self from a level of consciousness where, by a paradox, it somehow already exists. Teachers call this the Eternal Now.

When he enters the Third Heaven before reincarnating again, the pilgrim has to endeavour to implant deep within his consciousness as much as he can as yet absorb of this image of his future self. What he absorbs will be the fruit of intuition – tuition from within – bringing to him an instant inner recognition. There begin to open up new perceptions which are like spiritual seeds which later will come to flower on earth. These perceptions are of archetypal spiritual qualities. In his past lives he has so far realised only a very imperfect fragment of them. He must become sufficiently perfected to be lived through by these qualities whilst on earth. In something of the way in which a great composer is lived through by his artistic creations, so will the pilgrim gradually be lived through by perfect qualities of which in future lives he will become more and more the willing servant.

3

In what way do the soul events which the pilgrim has formerly sown within himself now limit him in the Third Heaven? Let us suppose that in his most recent life he had brought to earth ideals of philanthropy which he set about expressing, but that other considerations – prudence, self-interest, desire for praise, coldness or lack of imaginative participation in the true needs of others – intervened and partially blinded him, closing his heart where it most needed to be open. His purgation will have enabled him to see where he fell short. As he moves gradually towards living in the higher elements of his being and, in doing so, moves into the Third Heaven, he will receive, in an archetypal form, a glimpse of ideas of philanthropy as they are known by beings higher in the hierarchy who ray these down to him. But his philanthropic lacks on earth (along with his other lacks) will have shortened the range of the archetypal ideas to which he can as yet respond, and which otherwise would have been open to him to receive. Thus what he himself is, the consciousness which he has created over many earth lives, limits the depth to which he can penetrate into the Third Heaven. Therein lies the immense importance of what he achieved, or failed to achieve, on earth. Had his stature been larger, he would now see further, would be able to receive from further up the scale of being. In this sense his past is holding him back.

This is an exceedingly difficult area in which to be able to feel we know correctly what the laws of the afterlife really are. Certain teachers, including Rudolf Steiner, affirm that it is only on earth that new values can be built permanently into the character; through revisiting the earth the failure can be made up and overcome by strenuous work. Man is allowed a joyful participation in the vision shown to him in the Third Heaven in archetypal form. But it is the worldly part which when next reincarnated must be transformed so that the soul succeeds in firmly planting on earth what had been neglected before.

Later on, when this particular man is reborn to earth, he will find himself inwardly urged, he hardly knows why, to fulfil philanthropic ideals which belong, it seems to him, to the very innermost of his being. He sets his heart towards this as if his very honour depends upon it. In a very real way it does. He is making up ground on earth and also in preparation for the next interim period between his earth lives. As he succeeds, it will entitle him, when he dies, to move further than before into an understanding of the archetypal philanthropic impulses which once more he will meet. He will become entitled to share these more intimately and with greater insight than formerly, and when he has done so, he will then in turn in his next life be able to express them on earth more perfectly than in his present life.

This, however, will not make up the whole of the programme devised for this next life. Other difficulties will rise up, for deep within him are still likely to lie the results of opportunities lost in earlier lives, bunglings in a different part of his being, and characteristics still infant in degree and never developed. These will form part of the cross he will carry in the new life, his thorns in the flesh, some probably quite separate from all that makes up his philanthropy, some probably biting deeply and corrosively into it. As with most men, he will still be his own worst enemy; and all that is his enemy he will have to try to recreate, so that it becomes his friend, and the friend of the world as well.

4

Life in the Second and Third Heavens resembles the fairy story of the sleeping princess awakened by her rescuer. The princess represents the imprisoned soul, the rescuing prince who claims her represents the spirit. The tangle through which the prince must penetrate is made up of the false values of earth and the imprisoning errors of past lives. Now the soul learns to resume something more of the grand plan intended for it, much of which was lost or departed from when on earth.

In this archetypal world of the Third Heaven, in Rudolf Steiner's categorisation, there are cradled the inspirations of the social reformer, of the philanthropist, of those in the great healing vocations, of teachers and of preachers, of scientific discovery and invention, of creative art in every form – all those human activities which serve to nourish the inward part of man. In this world there come to him realisations, comparatively perfect in form, which he finds blissful to contemplate; but at this level he is mindful always that to receive demands in turn many subsequent acts of service. That is why these creative ideas are not a complete fulfilment in themselves, until man, by planting them in the earth, has fully made them his own.

This is perhaps part of what Blake means when he says that eternity is in love with the productions of time. In order to fulfil these creative ideas and to give them their full sense and meaning, reincarnation has to be faced. There is no easy heaven, and such heaven as is won must soon be left again; man is a child of earth for a very long period indeed, and must constantly return to it.

5

A multitude of these creative and archetypal ideas are described as flowing continuously through the group leader and other beings at exalted level. These are not fixed concepts but a constant interweaving and activisation, like a living stream which continually pours forth ever-changing fountains of water and yet at its source remains itself. It is indicated that these ideas are in reality woven out of the minds of other still higher beings who are themselves at the command and disposal of ineffable beings above them; they are operating at a level of consciousness which, however high to us, to them represents a descent into material expression. These beings do not come or need to come down into the clay of matter as do those still tied by earth.

The traveller, having experienced many of the travails of soul life with its emotional and mental joys and sorrows, faces more closely the sacred and innermost part of himself – his spirit, as distinct from his soul and body. We are getting now into rarefied areas. Here perhaps the theologians 'eternal life' is found. Within every man, we are told, is the tiny spark of divinity, in which lies the seed image created by the supreme force and which it is for man himself, over an infinitely long period, to actualise and to make into that flower of himself which already exists in the mind of divinity. This is man's sacred collaboration, to make himself by deeds that which he potentially is. As he advances through the mental worlds, insight becomes immediate; he absorbs simply by being.

Nothing is more striking than the uniformity of agreement between men of all races and at all times in describing mystical experience. They continually speak of awareness of the unity of all life, their union with it and the freedom of finding oneself at one with all that the universe contains. To many, the picture is of momentarily sharing a fragment of the Christ consciousness, Christ the overlord of the cosmic system in which we live; a reaching out to and touching the hem of His consciousness. Of this, the mystics, their words inevitably failing, convey as much by non-saying as by saying. They say, like the poet : 'Alas, and is not mine a language dead?'

On some very distant day the choice becomes available, when a man has paid his uttermost debt to the earth, to decide for himself whether he will dare the final bound and become cast upon the divine stream which will lead him away for ever from earth incarnations and further towards the Divine Principle. This may be some of the meaning behind the Christian concept of the mystical marriage : the individual soul is absorbed into the spirit, and what it becomes then is a mystery.

Man feels reluctant and fearful towards the idea of becoming taken up into something other and greater than himself, and this idea is often resisted for a long time.

The traveller's other course is, instead, to choose to hold back and cling to some smaller felicity. Few, F. W. H. Myers found, are 'strong enough to make the great leap'. Some lofty ones, however, from quite different motives, acting not from a necessity of smallness but through a loving sacrifice, do choose to take upon themselves again some of the burdens of the world and remain to help others up the slow rungs of the spiritual ladder. Such a choice, the choice of the Bodhisattva, the compassionate one, is far, far ahead for most of us, but, as a distant spiritual Everest, it must for brief moments be contemplated.

Within the individual, and similarly within the group itself, life holds this strange principle of growth. Whether through hardship and limitation, or whether by rejoicing in the Lord, growth results in the end. When its long purpose has been fulfilled, the group and all its members move on as a whole to some area of existence outside the earth planet. In the end one will have no meaning apart from the meaning which exists in the group, and before the face of the Lord. Thus are the essential needs of each one's nature met in the end, through grace, through joy and companionship but also through travail. Life after death in its further states leads us to mysteries, and though we may point towards these we must remain content essentially to leave them still in mystery.

It has become clear that an essential part of the overall picture presented from the discarnate world is that it treats reincarnation on to earth as a fact. A further look may tell us a little of how this process proves to be a nourishing and deeply valuable aid for the soul, before it is ready to scale the further heights.

PART THREE

Some Implications

CHAPTER 13

Reincarnation

1

It would be a shallow view which supposes that these discarnate accounts solve the many problems of existence. Nor must a wrong authority be attributed to them. There is no authority whatever in their merely coming from such a source – their only authority lies in whatever degree of internal coherence they possess. Nor, as we have seen, do the accounts necessarily all agree with one another. They cannot be expected to, and nowhere is this more true than in the subject of reincarnation. One therefore has to find an answer to the problem of how to compare communicators who declare that reincarnation is a truth and those on the contrary who swear it is not so, and say they have never met anybody who knows he has been reincarnated. Both kinds of account exist. Let us be more careful and more patient than to say that if they cancel one another out neither can be relied upon as being true. For it is quite clear that the material relating to reincarnation forms some of the most important information which has reached us of the nature of life after death.

In the great Eastern religions, of course, reincarnation is found everywhere; it has a very respectable history. Those who believe it in one form or another outnumber Christians; obviously mere numbers are no proof of its veracity, but included amongst believers are many Eastern religious thinkers of great metaphysical subtlety, as well as many holy mystics.

At first sight, the emergence of reincarnation as a prominent factor in these stories is surprising to Western minds, accustomed for long to an expectation of a single life, followed by an aftermath based on its consequences. Indeed, Western minds often start by rejecting the reincarnationist part of the post-mortem picture.

In several cases struggles have taken place over a number of years between mediums who violently rejected reincarnation – Mrs Estelle Roberts was one – and their trance communicators who believed it, and proceeded to continue to teach it, however distasteful their mediums found it. In the end the medium has usually come to accept the doctrine, but not always, and at times only very partially and reluctantly.

What are the most significant factors in this testimony pointing towards reincarnation? One is that those teachers who most clearly display wisdom and insight about other matters invariably do teach reincarnation and, as has been said, irrespective of their medium's own convictions. Those who ignore reincarnation on the whole have not produced in other respects material of similar insight. They cannot be said to be such good witnesses.

Much more important, however, is that the teaching accounts which record the traveller's further journeys require reincarnation to be true if they are to bear their full meaning. There is no doubt about it that in such accounts the *structure* of existence after death, its intellectual, emotional and spiritual intelligibility, depends upon it. It is the close-at-hand accounts, made soon after death, which usually do not introduce it, or vehemently deny it. True there are one or two speakers who claim to have lived a thousand years and have never met with reincarnation, but perhaps these, very much in the minority, are encapsulated, like the brethren of the Celtic Church, in old tenets.

2

Let us now look a little more closely, within the context of the accounts, at the linear or forward march view (one life), and the cyclical view (reincarnation).

Most discarnates who proclaim a forward march theory have not been able to give any effective picture beyond the First Heaven. This surely is significant.

The principal weakness of the theory is that the immortality it promises is held to be earned by the very slender work of seventy years or so of earth life. Any one life, even when apparently fulfilled, has so much left outside it, has so many sides of living which it has not touched, has never been called upon to face a number of problems, that the test would surely be incomplete if, from so brief a trial, immortality is to be gained.

The forward march picture suggests a certain ease of accomplishment. True, it tells of succour towards those who have just arrived upon discarnate shores, and succour also to those whose pain and grief call out from earth for help. Nevertheless, there appears here a fatal hint of a mutual congratulation society, where aid is shown as a voluntary undertaking from a superior position, whereas in the reincarnation picture it is emphatically the fulfilment of inescapable duty. One strength of the reincarnation picture lies in the unremitting responsibility it acknowledges towards life on earth; and still more, in the strenuous picture of having to return to earth in order to earn *there*, more than in the discarnate world, what is required to make the character more whole. Reincarnation calls for more than absentee do-gooders. It makes the next earth life the proving ground which sets the challenge : can character qualities, missed out before and since grown in the favourable horticultural nurseries of the hereafter, be grown firmly also in the impoverished soil of earth when the next opportunity comes? This concept of reincarnation is robust and astringent.

Reincarnation orients man both to earth and to post-mortem realms in a firm and organic way for, as a member of a spiritual group, his destiny and his struggle does not belong to him alone but forms part of a long and deeply rewarding set of relationships. For a long time his roots will still stretch downwards. He is a tree belonging equally to the earth, to the sky and to the forest all around him. However alien much in the universe may seem, his inward sense tells him that he has within his group a spiritual home which will never fail him. 'I am in you, ye are in me and we are in the Father.' Apart from what deeper meanings this holds, it also forms a statement of group relationships. The Father, in *one* aspect, can be looked up to as the far advanced leader round which members of the group cluster and from whom they draw much of their spiritual nourishment.

3

If reincarnation is part of the causal structure of events in discarnate life, as well as of those on earth, and if a life is but a chapter in a long story, then many injustices lose their sting. Inscrutable events and unaccountable emotions can be much more readily accepted if they relate to tasks and events in former lives, in the shape of old difficulties of character not resolved before, facets one had intended to, but then failed to, polish, debts to earth left unpaid.

Even though a man often cannot interpret the exact causality involved, it makes a great difference if he can accept that such causality does exist, rooted in his past, pointing towards a better development of his own future, or straightening some tangled threads of relationship formerly made awry. Then he can face with hardihood events which alternately lift him up, challenge him, or strike him down. It is a little like finding oneself dealt a hand of cards, in some cases a good hand, in others a bad hand, but where each card dealt is directly related to events arising out of characteristics which the holder of the hand has formerly built within himself.

4

A longer story than that of a single life best explains those deep and sometimes overmastering impulses otherwise seemingly planted so unfairly in a character. A man will liberate himself from himself more willingly once he knows his difficulties of temperament flow from a former life of his own. The principle applies whether his temperament is inherited from his present parents or else springs up seemingly in defiance of genetic law. Certain parents are appropriate because they can implant in their child the characteristics his destiny needs. He then takes from them what, in a very real sense, is already his. In other cases he can appear a changeling to his own parents, with characteristics which they cannot identify either in themselves or in the training they have given him, parts which arise and contradict their local setting. The unknown preceding chapters have set in motion much of the plot, which otherwise can seem so unfair and so mysterious.

5

If all men must perfect themselves, does this imply that eventually every man must be an Admirable Crichton, completely rounded and equipped for every task, so that all would resemble one another like peas? Not so, for though individual weaknesses must be overcome, each soul remains unique. What is required appears to be a basic equipment of response, a fundamental set of resources, together with the particular, more specific and specialised spiritual attributes needed for the tasks set within the group to which the soul belongs. Reincarnation gives meaning, or at least a firm promise of a long-term meaning, to the vocational mystery of each earth life. So many find themselves confronting unwelcome yet unavoidable tasks, which intrude themselves into the life pattern and seem the very opposite of what each would have chosen. This is most usually due to karmic bonds to be set straight between man and man, or arises from things springing from what had been left undone or done crookedly before. But this is not always so. It need not necessarily be based on ancient failings or guilt. The seeming burden can also spring from the principle of compassion. It may be an opportunity for the ultimately joyous creation of good karma. Tasks in life look forward as well as backward. The purpose can be to bestow new help, not help already owed from the past – for instance by marriage to one who, it has been foreseen by the helper before his or her life began, will suffer after marriage years of crippledom, ill health, or even insanity. The bargain, in spiritual result, may not be so one-sided as it appears. There may be mutual contributions and gains. The two may belong to the same spiritual group.

There can be the placing of a man in a sour and ill favoured soil when in more sunny ground he would never have succeeded in growing certain tendrils of the soul, the need for which he had failed to see until, through hardship, they began to spring forth, bringing unexpected beauty to his shape. With acceptance of the reincarnation picture, many strands come to convey their own purpose as they are lived out. These bring a much enhanced conviction of meaning behind all life, however inscrutable much of it still appears.

On the earth we live as it were on the dark side of the moon; with the reincarnationist picture a growing sense arises that the moon indeed has a bright side, and that the two together form an integral part of one circle. Reincarnation fills life with service of a kind which is meaningful within a larger pattern; where opportunity and debt can best be seen as opposite sides of the same coin. Servitude is no longer so when it becomes turned to service. Reincarnational tasks can often be happy and fruitful continuations. One returns with the fruits of old achievement just as frequently as with debts. Again, there is good karma as well as bad karma.

6

As long as a man lives only in his outer personality, he is in something of a prison, ceaselessly acting and reacting to every circumstance; reincarnation is an important tool which puts into his hands clues which can lead him past the sensory maze and forwards towards his essential being. Intuitions can arise, almost as if they are memories, pointing to the true pattern which his outer personality is of itself too short-sighted to grasp.

It is, of course, very difficult to understand how the various lives and personalities which a man has gone through are inwardly related. The present reincarnation picture is almost certainly too simple. Subleties are sensed to lie behind the scene, beyond our grasp at present. The more delicate indications in these imperfectly glimpsed accounts point away from a man simply returning to his next life, lock, stock and barrel. Instead he brings back only certain aspects of himself, in order that he can concentrate intensively on perfecting these particular traits. His own higher self forms the link between these varying earth lives.

Thus a man will have acquired, through each succeeding life, a number of selves of his own, and we have seen that the outer shell of each of these personalities, the costume part, when played and finished is ultimately cast away at the second death; and that the essence of what was learned whilst wearing that costume is preserved within the higher though still incomplete self.

So we have, first, the outer, costume self, a man's earth personality, which continues for a while and which he may cling to but will abandon when he has outgrown it. And, second, the inner, total self, which he regains or rejoins and which has facets both polished and unpolished. This is the causal self. It takes him much hard work to rediscover and rejoin this self. Partial access to it is possible on earth. As he moves upward through realms of consciousness he recognises that his unworked-on facets cannot as yet take sufficient of the light; he longs to grow the equipment which will enable him to reflect and express more of spiritual reality. So he returns to earth with a double task. First to polish a new facet in himself so as to act out, as far as he can, upon the earth the aspect of perfection he saw as an archetype in those now once again distant upper realms of consciousness. Also he brings back legacies from former costume selves.

The seeds stored in his causal self, some of which are replanted in his next earth life in order to produce a richer harvest, now confront him, often as inner weaknesses and also in the shape of outer events, bringing exacting pressures he cannot escape. The bread he formerly cast upon the waters returns to him, as difficulties to be resolved or as gifts and opportunities seemingly unearned. This is the meaning of the stories of Pandora's box, and of the gifts of the good and bad fairies at the christening. Thus he has both high and low tasks and this makes up the complex troubled being who finds himself again upon earth, whose very first utterance is a cry.

7

Reincarnation is an essentially shapely idea and gives sense to some of the more baffling problems in life. Many persons of sensibility confront the bleaker events in life as one confronting a blank and high wall – cancer in a child, natural disasters, the cruelties of war, the sufferings of the apparently innocent – and these make it impossible for them to conceive of any just God. That there is a further life beyond this one to which these sufferers will be translated is one factor which ameliorates some of the worst seeming injustice, but without removing more than a part of it. The fundamental blows of fate remain, even if now seen as not being final.

Reincarnation lightens the picture a little more, for to the idea of a continuation after death is added a causality extending far beyond the immediate event. What if a thing seen formerly as a final event is only a single episode, like a bead upon a necklace, the meaning lying in the necklace, not the bead? One's compassion, if it is for the victim alone, can be misleading: a slaughter, a fatal illness, is a composite event; the slayer and the mourners each have their role to play, their lesson to learn. The victim may really be the one best off. In the total pattern he could be more willing than he seems.

Seeming injustice can persuade a man to revert to a selfishness into which he otherwise would not lapse, and which his inner nature can tell him is certainly wrong.

Yet, irrespective of beliefs, many both on earth and beyond have found that suffering endured has brought them fruits of more value than joy, or than life on an even keel; to them, seeming injustice has been replaced by an inner gain. A reincarnationist ceases to cry out against an unjust God, for he accepts a causality which stretches both before and after the event and which, if accepted, can enrich the unhappy event itself.

Reincarnation lends deeper understanding of why so many earth relationships, whether happy or unhappy in their results, seem so compulsive. Whether apparently arising from personality factors or through pressure of circumstance, they become too strong to be resisted, for some of them result from deep bonds, for good or ill, created in the past. Old enmities and injuries of the soul have to be repaired, sometimes through what can be, in happier circumstances, the most fruitful and happy of human relationships – friendship, love, marriage, the family – but which, when now recreated awry or later turned awry, present a difficult opportunity to overcome the past.

This often arises in the form of a sacrifice, often unwilling, often resented bitterly as an unfair bond. A daughter condemned to forego marriage to look after an elderly mother can be one example. Love and hate at the level of personal emotion are, after all, close together and either may turn into the other. Yet if it comes to be sensed that the real purpose of such a union between two persons springs from a deep knot to be unravelled, then, through acceptance, the burden of the mutual task to be accomplished can become lighter. To bear one's lot and not rail against it brings important fruits.

On the other hand, if old relationships have been happy and fulfilled in an earlier life then, when resumed in a new incarnation, they can take on a deepened impulse towards impersonal service, the carrying out of unselfish, outward-going tasks. The link becomes felt by those involved as something larger and other than personal attachment. If the bond arises through common membership of the spiritual group, the link will be at bottom a soul companionship. Difficulties at personality level then come to be of less account. This companionship of soul is not exclusive to two persons or a small group but basically extends to the whole spiritual family of which these form part; many of whom cannot be known whilst on earth, for all will not be in incarnation at that particular time. Such a companionship must never be diminished into an exclusive spiritual clique.

When one is perhaps baffled by circumstances, not knowing where to turn, deeply uncertain of one's purpose and lot in life, then one's deeper intuitions can be sharpened by acceptance of reincarnation. Though of course these can be misinterpreted or overlaid, they can point to the main purposes of the particular incarnation. Then, however lonely his lot – and indeed at stages in the spiritual path it is, and indeed must be, lonely – a man never feels completely alone any more; he is sustained by knowing that his spiritual group exists, even though few members seem to be around him on earth and contact with those beyond may be dim and uncertain. To accept the existence of his group soul lends fortitude and endurance when these qualities are otherwise hardest to come by, and in happier days brings a sustaining joy. He comes to feel he is indeed walking along his proper spiritual path.

8

It is often asked whether we are free to choose to reincarnate or not. Some accounts say a choice is open. Deeper ones suggest that there may seem to be a choice, but when the issue is truly seen reincarnation is inevitable. Perhaps an element of choice exists in being able to delay somewhat the moment of return until the person feels more ready. Very unevolved men and women, with little spiritual understanding, are likely to be returned into incarnation very soon, simply because after death their perceptions cannot take them far. They have less scope. Being near to earth consciousness, they will return soon because they can learn better there. However, to attempt to judge a man's spiritual stature merely by his earth circumstances is very unwise. The inner man can belie the outer. A peasant may be much further on, in terms of spiritual wisdom, than the intellectual who confidently despises him.

As to the time which elapses between one incarnation and the next, no figure can be laid down. Surely it will depend upon a process of learning which will be very different for different people. Reincarnation will come about when the time is ripe. This is an area where estimates are often given. It is unwise to rely on them. The more dogmatically information is given, the more unreliable it is likely to be.

9

A perennial question asked by opponents of reincarnation is: why then do we not remember our past lives?'. The answer is that many do remember, although usually only in a fragmentary way. What is thus recalled, however, invariably needs a spiritual interpretation if proper use is to be made of it; usually it points unmistakably to a lesson or difficulty in the present life situation.

Many probably possess the delicate receptive antennae necessary to pick up such reincarnational intimations but are not patient enough to let these come in their own time, as they must. Instead they demand reincarnation memories in a ready form and at their behest – and they expect flattering ones at that! But, as with other spiritual things, the coming of reincarnation memories first has to be earned, through the spiritual detachment and sensitivity needed for their reception or else, if presented by discarnate teachers, they must be paid for later by being utilised fruitfully to achieve the tasks, probably difficult ones, now facing that individual.

These are quite different from the glamorous 'reincarnation memories' often rightly scoffed at by the sceptical. True memories are very, very seldom at any glamorous personality level. There are plenty of claimants around for the personalities of Cleopatra, Marie-Antoinette or Nefertiti, but who learns anything from supposing that they were once these beings? Stupid people may like to think they were Cleopatra, but this is of no consequence and has no bearing on true ancient memories. A fairly sure test of a true reincarnation memory is whether it points to a past or a present failure. A past life of earthly pride and apparent achievement, if indeed it is correctly remembered, will be likely to show in a later life its reverse and unresolved side of selfishness, hate and cruelty upon which part of its misleading glories may have been based, and these now will be its legacies to be faced and put right.

Whilst it is sound to look on reincarnation in terms of debts, unhappinesses, and what, if they were not so just, one might falsely call punishments, it is equally important not to overlook other happier though unglamorous threads: the purpose of events and meetings is not only to redress, it is also to enhance, and take forward what has been commenced in earlier days. Thus one meets persons who have a particularly beneficent influence upon one: some seem to put tools into one's hands which have been lacking before; others open doors of opportunity, bring forward and help to develop, perhaps out of a love relationship, new talents and gifts or more shapely characteristics. Whether for seeming ill or certain good, relationships all belong to a blessed brotherhood of purpose, a brotherhood of opportunity. Reincarnation is essentially opportunity.

CHAPTER 14

Summing Up

1

In comparatively modern times a number of structured schemes
have been produced which picture man's journey through post-
mortem regions – by Swedenborg, Madame Blavatsky, Rudolf
Steiner, Max Heindel, R. W. Lees, Dr Crookall; by the
amanuensis of 'Oahspe'; and after their deaths by Arthur Conan
Doyle and Frederic Myers. There are, as well, many more
fragmentary pictures in Spiritualistic writings. These schematic
statements are undoubtedly of considerable value in clarifying
the nature of post-mortem experience, but if they take on too
unyielding a form they can become misleading. Although a
number of correspondences exist between these schemes, any
attempt to collate them in a formal, logical way reveals apparent
discrepancies. The reason is clear: the authors of these various
schemes were certainly not working from one common level of
spiritual awareness; as consciousness deepens, the picture widens.
What is appropriate when seen from one level of consciousness
becomes less so when seen from another, deeper one. Then, too,
the subtle path of growth of an individual living being must
inevitably elude at times a complete adherence to the rigid
forms and patterns which the intellect seeks to impose. Post-
mortem life does not consist of passing through a number of
watertight areas in a regular and invariable manner, though
many interpret the accounts to make it seem so.

Different men learn in different ways. Within post-mortem life as a whole, and by this is meant the seemingly very limited area of it within the three heavens, it is clearly of no consequence what level of awareness a man has reached at any particular time, nor how long he chooses to linger there. Nor, because one man has reached some level to which a superior label can be attached, and another is bound up in some area which bears an inferior name, does it mean that the one man is better than the other. All are equal in the great scheme. To progress 'faster' than another is an illusory statement. Each man deals with what is in front of him in post-mortem life until he has absorbed its lesson and its meaning and is at all times held securely within the palm of God, as an infinitely small fragment of the creative life force.

2

It would hardly be useful to include yet another scheme, another necessarily oversimplified structure. Hence the plan of the book has been instead to draw together a number of typical experiences and to try to describe something of the areas of consciousness they reflect, as far as we can understand these at present. It is hoped that enough has been provided for most readers to find something which strikes significantly upon their own private sense of reality. If one ponders upon these accounts and comes eventually to accept some of them as reports of genuine experience, however incomplete, they will become guide-posts to some of the 'many mansions'. In time, other people will add new guide-posts and a picture will gradually arise a little closer to the real situation. Meanwhile, we have to be content with explorers' trails over an only partly known country. Schematic statements are the corresponding maps and are bound to be faulty or misleading, however honourably constructed. These maps are incomplete. Hence it can become confusing if they are laid, like tracings, one upon the other.

For instance, take the matter of the second death. Arthur Conan Doyle describes it as a decisive event at the point of change between the Summerland and the Mental World : his Summerland and First Heaven overlap. Myers calls the second death 'the breaking of the image', marking transition between what he names the fourth and fifth stages. It is not always easy to distinguish the levels of consciousness represented by Myers's spheres. Madame Blavatsky speaks of the casting away of the 'shell' at the level of the Lower Manas (personal mind) and the emergence of the 'butterfly' at the level of the Higher Manas (spiritual mind), almost as if it were an automatic event. Frances Banks, on the other hand, 'rejoins her soul' without telling us of any decisive experience of a second death, but more as a gradual acclimatisation and stepping up of her consciousness. Pauchard, very soon after his death, meets with *scoriae* but does not describe a second death as such, though towards the end of his book he prepares to expand to a consciousness where, he is told, he will see into his former lives. The three descriptions quoted in Chapter 9 of transition through the second death are each set within a somewhat differing scheme, yet each is unmistakably describing the same event.

Ancient Egyptian and ancient and modern Tibetan accounts present a somewhat terrifying picture of overall irrevocable consequences, as if acts committed in life will condemn a man to an unalterable future after death. Such heavily overcast scenes suggest the colouring of priestcraft, especially where the future is claimed to depend upon rites carried out by others at the time of death. So often in history priests have sought power over men through fear. Nor has this been absent in Christian threats of hell-fire, whether medieval or later. In Victorian times, some pictures of Winterland were coloured (whether by communicator or recipient) by a self-righteousness unlikely to be felt now. Quite other, for instance, is the compassion in Frances Banks's picture. Communicators have gradually overcome and laid aside concepts which to their recipients of nearly a hundred years ago formed part of the general fabric of religious thought. In recent accounts, as we have seen, the idea of punishment is replaced by that of impersonal consequences and of re-education and rehabilitation.

Nevertheless, in spite of differences of attribution or of emphasis, a picture emerges which does unquestionably point to an overall spiritual plan, though almost certainly not in the neat but somewhat rigid order which rational attention prefers and expects.

3

Let us look at the general implications which arise from this composite material.

At the beginning of the book it was said of post-mortem accounts that no guarantee or formal proof can reside in them. Their acceptance as broadly truthful accounts lies in the judgement of each reader : does he find them convincing as pictures of human experiences? Has T. E. Lawrence overcome twisted factors in his earth character? Is Frances Banks gradually becoming a larger being than the one who resumed her nun's garments immediately after death? Is Pauchard's mind continually modifying itself in the light of further ideas? Did Mrs Willett, as a result of her posthumous review, indeed come to see more clearly the emotional wilfulness she had borne towards her son? Did she in repenting thereby deepen her post-mortem love for him? Has Arthur Conan Doyle revised part of his earth valuation of Spiritualism, which he had preached so forcefully and in a missionary spirit? After his death he says he found many communications to be less valid and accurate than he had supposed, and this disquieted him. Oliver Lodge, as will be quoted, reports a much-enhanced appreciation of spiritual guides and teachers. Both of these communicators are self-critical of their earth concepts. One reports an overvaluation and the other an undervaluation.

Do many discover that faults and virtues brought over from earth now need to be quite differently assessed? Above all, when the accounts are put together, do they paint a picture of a continuing life which is challenging and demanding?

If the general picture presented in communications adds up

to something which is more realistic and more satisfying, and in spite of its imperfections more convincing than the standard pictures from orthodox sources, then it is worthy of very serious consideration.

4

If inquiry into the nature of life after death were only to consist of an anticipatory look forward, it could be little more than curiosity. However, it is by no means a matter of reading the final chapters of a book before reaching the middle ones, still less a crib unlawfully giving information we are not yet intended to have. It calls much more for the kind of questions an explorer asks before he embarks upon an important expedition. What mental equipment will be required? What lacks or weaknesses has he which are likely to obstruct him at a certain stage of the journey and prevent him from moving forward? Any explorer worth his salt tries to anticipate every possible difficulty and provide for it. The explorer of the afterlife who will one day find himself embarked on his journey, perhaps suddenly and involuntarily, can meanwhile come to recognise that it is the life pattern he is now daily creating in himself that will become his explorer's equipment then. His temper is completely different from those who so often declare : 'We are not meant to explore', 'We would have been told if we are meant to know', or 'It is enough to know when the time comes'. We *can* know at least something now. We *are* being told.

Nobody, after all, would suggest that it is wrong to try to discover the moral laws governing mankind on earth, or that pollution must be allowed to occur before trying to do anything to lessen it, or that preventive medicine is unlawful. If a little insight into moral laws can be imparted by those who have preceded us into death, is it not natural and lawful that they should relate their discoveries, much in the spirit in which a father might instruct his son? Indeed, such sharing can surely be a part of the communion of souls.

Essentially the material brings about alterations both in one's time scale and one's scale of values. One becomes able to take a longer view of existence. Instead of a gulf between life as it is lived on earth and life as it may (or may not) exist beyond, a picture gradually arises of an inner world to which men belong *both* before and after death, and in which the same spiritual laws hold good there as here. This is the key concept: that an inner world exists; that men and women already belong to it, can get to know some of its laws and can act accordingly.

It is then for each man to judge whether by so doing he gradually becomes a better earth citizen. He is free to apply this test or not as he wishes, but it is a realistic test.

5

The distance, in terms of spiritual knowledge, which the traveller covers between one life and another is comparatively short.

> . . . He gradually comes to realise the remoteness of those into whose hands the ultimate destiny of stars and planets is entrusted. In other words, he comes to perceive that the celestial hierarchy extends to heights which he can scarcely conceive, and that the fate of humanity on this particular globe is determined in the last resort by the decisions made by beings who dwell in realms into which even highly developed spirits cannot in their present condition penetrate. And this impels him to still greater humility and conscientiousness in the carrying out of the tasks which have been assigned to him by those directing his development.[1]

The further the pilgrim goes, the harder he clearly finds it to convey what his extended spiritual perceptions have begun to to show him. Meanwhile those in the immediate beyond, like those who are treading early steps on the spiritual path on earth, usually suppose themselves to have got much further along the road than they really have. They still measure spiritual things by an earthly yardstick. Concepts are crystallised too easily and too soon. The more experienced narrator emphasises that his picture is a fragment of the full reality, which he knows is far beyond his own powers of understanding.

6

To find meaning in one's earth life grows even more important once the pilgrim realises that existence ahead is very long indeed. Its very length makes it likely to be more than an aftermath determined entirely by what has gone on in the extremely short space of a single lifespan, this one term in a very serious kindergarten school. More advanced lessons are available on earth to those willing to pay their cost and win through to a change of consciousness. On the other hand many classes soon after death are no more than belated kindergarten ones intended for earth. It will be hard to find that these kindergarten lessons could with more profit have been learned here.

Betty, a sensitive who worked in a fully conscious way, reports a telepathic lesson on how best to live on earth:

The way they are showing me seems so difficult and painful – the skeleton dragged from the living body. . . . They are showing it to me and saying: This is the real structure. All the rest, your flesh, your clothes, your belongings, the motor you ride in – you just pile on yourself. But after all there's your real structure that has to carry all the unnecessary stuff. Yet nobody wants to walk around in his skeleton. But you can entirely clothe it in something better than all that smothering stuff . . . My, that other stuff looks clumsy, piled up all around; looks like Mrs Tanner's [a very wealthy acquisitive woman] stuff. It's repellent. It positively nauseates me. I wouldn't like to get back into that! As they take it away I feel so naked and cold. It is rather terrible to have it taken away; almost acute suffering. Oh, wait! I don't know what I'm going to do. I don't know where to begin. Oh, my! – there's a little something gathering about me, rather thin and filmy, not formed and finished. I don't think that was a nice symbol. I don't feel as much at home as I did in all that nice warm cosy Tanner stuff. I'm all new and self-conscious and a little cold. – Yes, I see what you mean. – These strange exercises just separate me before my eyes; take out parts of me and set them aside; and discard the rest. . . .

But these smothery things are all so warm and human – You can go on living in the smothery things if you want to; and there's no direct harm and no judgment held against you for it. Then why all this effort in this life? The answer is: It is inexorably true that it has got to be done some time, that great passionate shove has to be done some time. Each one must struggle and free himself; there is no escape; it is the law; and the longer you procrastinate and delay, the harder that struggle is going to be and the softer and more unfit for it you are going to be. It will be a terrible state, suffering discouragement, blackness if you delay. Delay bears too heavy interest. That is why all this exhortation for this life, why they don't wait until we go over there. This life *is* that tearing out of your skeleton, and when we are not doing it here, now, we are making it *so* much harder for ourselves later. This is our crucial moment of struggle right now. How blind and stupid to say wait for such things until we get over! That is what your incarnation here is – your test. That is what they have been trying to tell us . . . We can take the easier way, but it delays the game and makes it harder. Use every ounce in you, for you are bound to clump and get soft again.[2]

The immediate earth curriculum is clearly shaped to the pupil. Humans are not all in the same class, even though in the same classroom. The intricate pattern of life will quite certainly put a man in the way of learning just those things spiritually necessary for him to learn; his post-mortem review shows him how necessarily and how justly these sometimes unwelcome things came to him. Whilst on earth he has, of course, the power of refusing to learn, thus choosing to be a dunce at his own most important task. Tasks, however, are much more than the result of being in a penitentiary; they are often very creative. Life is more than a moral lesson; one learns to live also with joy. Nor is joy necessarily absent when very difficult tasks and roles present themselves.

The mufflings and shackles become of less consequence when life can be lived with clearer concentration on its real issues. The personal pace of living speeds up as access is gained to the inner world of perception pointing to the deeper truths of relationships, to the companionship of the spirit, and also offering an impersonal philosophy. The blows which face the outer personality, when rightly accepted, prove to be a striking off of shackles. Life becomes more invigorating as men begin to bathe in the radiant energies which flow down from level to level of the hierarchy.

The whole universe, as every word of discarnate communication proclaims, is sustained by love, however inadequate the acts of men on earth. Then ceases the cry of harsh inequality, of unfair discrimination, or of a God who cannot exist because He doesn't seem to behave as humans, from their position in the kindergarten class, expect Him to. Apparent injustice can look very different to a man willing to accept that his particular lessons are not an arbitrary ruling from a godhead but instead are to be found deep in his own total nature. The lessons are really painting his own portrait.

Yet the earth is more than a schoolroom to be left rapidly behind on death. It is also a workshop, a desert, a local anarchy; but, as well, a neglected kingdom which will one day blossom as the rose.

7

A highly important element in the story is that men are not thrown into earth life and left alone. How can the kindergarten pupils learn their lessons without a teacher or a number of teachers? Life itself, of course, is an important part of the teaching process, and the pupils also teach one another, sometimes without knowing they are doing so.

But if the design is more intricate still, if indeed no sparrow falls unheeded, then the complex process of bringing people together, of helping events come to pass, must surely be directed in part by beings of superior intelligence. How is it that one meets the right person at the right time, that a spark is kindled merely through a passing contact? We must accept that a good deal of planning takes place behind the scenes, to bring together, say, a man and a woman, who hold towards each other both an unpaid debt and a strengthening joy, at a particular and appropriate time in the life of both. One cannot see how it has been brought to pass, but one can see how necessary the situation proves itself to be; how appropriate and even inevitable.

It is true, of course, that any such interweaving of inner and outer life must produce a paradox of tension: on the one hand the seeker is on the path alone; on the other hand, he is fundamentally one with his companions of the spirit, incarnate and discarnate. The paradox is resolved when he accepts that the task is his, the help is theirs. He has his private and local task within a wider design. To each man, it is said, a special teacher is allotted – his spiritual teacher, who will draw close if the man on earth permits it, who will speak to him in his innermost dreams and ideals, in his flashes of intuition, in moral compulsions which the one on earth recognises but cannot always explain; and who will also speak to him at times through his pupil's direct telepathic sensitivity, or through the help of a sensitive, or sometimes through ideas which seem to waken of themselves in the pupil's own mind.

Such a framework lends tone colours of a fascinating kind to the complex relationship between the discarnate teacher and his charge. The teacher will be found to be less concerned with the outer earth personality than with the long-term inner self. Why, it will be asked, cannot this inner self do all that is required without need of any independent teacher? Pauchard speaks of one part of the situation:

> . . . The true guide is within ourselves. Only in our present state of evolution we, generally, can neither hear nor see and so the superior I in us attracts one of his kind to make a bridge. He uses a delegate.[3]

The teacher or delegate speaks when the outer man cannot hear or will not listen deeply enough for himself. But the inner self does not live in isolation; it too drinks from the general stream of wisdom. Whether it is the teacher talking or his own inner self prompting him, the message will basically be the same, leading away from the outer personality and towards a larger self, towards more impersonal horizons.

However much alone in his moments of deep spiritual testing, and undoubtedly there are many such moments in the spiritual life, the pupil will come to know that his vision is gradually lengthening; he will begin to feel at last that he is at home in the universe and with its inhabitants in a way quite impossible when life is lived at personality level only. All this enriches him whilst on earth.

It will be objected that if all have such guides at hand their work will often be pointless and wasted, since so few humans have any knowledge of them. It is true that guides say that if, after long trial, they can make no impact, they withdraw, at least for a while. After his death, Oliver Lodge, communicating through Gladys Osborne Leonard, gave his own altered view on guides:

. . . He is told that these same instructors, teachers, will watch over him when he comes back to the earth, and that if he should be willing and attain a sense of unity with them, believe in them . . . that if he will react to that he will find himself in touch with these same leaders . . . He will most probably have them introduced to him as the Guides. I remember hearing far too much about the Guides at several of my earlier sittings. In fact, I was rather bored with the Guides. But now I understand, I understand; I have met them and I have recognised them as old-time friends, friends from a very long time ago, and I appreciate, I deeply appreciate, their faithfulness and their patience with me.[4]

8

Men and women very often feel that the familiar relationships which arise through love, parenthood, work, duty, vocation, are never on earth quite fulfilled to their depths. Always there is more than can be expressed, more that could have been done, more that could be understood and grasped and worked for. The limitation itself is a hint of the continuing and interwoven nature of true relationships; it is as if only part of the tale is told in a single life. Then the existence of long-term companions from former lives becomes more easily acceptable.

Speculation suggests that in the early lives of an individual, when its first small spiritual tendrils are being put out, problems are comparatively simple. Hard work of a physical kind, with much repetition, is well equated to the scale of the accompanying brain and consciousness. The peasant life is certainly one of discipline, but the discipline is largely from external necessities, toil for food and shelter. As the soul develops over many lives, more interior types of lesson are needed; different facets of the diamond begin to be polished.

We could in theory visualise a series of reincarnations in which a new facet is perfectly polished in each life. But of course it is not so. In all lives a constant dragging of the feet occurs. We know so well, too, how uneven lives are; how much that is admirable rubs cheek by jowl with what is ugly or even degraded. The man is thrust against that most unwelcome neighbour, the one who is inside him and part of himself; he does not like him, nor does he succeed in controlling his actions.

It seems clear that the plan is not for the whole of the self to come back each time, and that more can be achieved by a limitation of tasks and with it a closer attention to growing qualities immediately needed. As to the burden of handicaps from the past, it would be reasonable if only part is thrust upon a man at one time : the weight of his whole past might crush him altogether. Success and failure in any worldly sense now becomes totally irrelevant to the real meaning of any particular life. Each man has to recognise from deep within himself the tasks he needs to accomplish.

Everyone's character, it is clear, contains neglected corners, and it is a wholly logical necessity that these must be filled in during a later life. The facet to polish may be a very small one, yet extremely difficult for that particular temperament. On the other hand, qualities already well possessed may have to be left out in one incarnation because not needed for the immediate task in hand. The individual, in his whole being, may be much superior to this limited presentation of himself with which he temporarily has to live.

Earth facts can thus hide the true spiritual situation. Frances Banks declares the one looked upon as an enemy in life may have entered it in order to draw forth what is most valuable for the other to learn and may, indeed, in reality be a deeply advanced member of the same soul group and therefore really a dearly loved companion.

Obviously then it is impossible to know enough to become one another's keepers. To quote a discarnate teacher: 'You on earth *cannot* judge a man's life. We dare not judge it.'

9

The extended life view painted in many discarnate accounts thus points to overlapping spiritual factors woven into the individual life pattern. (1) Obstacles deeply embedded in the private temperament. (2) Karmic situations which have to be resolved, involving other persons. (3) The general opportunity for enrichment of the soul by experience on earth. (4) The larger plan from spiritual sources which men have come to earth to concretise and fulfil.

In this multiple situation, personal initiative, advice from spiritual sources and the welling up of knowledge from within the inner self are subtly interblended. The veil between inner and outer becomes thinner as men and women deepen their awareness; in their growing spiritual strength, karma itself can come to offer more of its lighter and joyful aspect. Souls begin to remember better their true nature. Every man can gradually become in part his own priest and find his task more intelligible as the voice of his deeper self is recognised.

10

Both on earth and beyond a man will not be all of a piece; part of himself will operate intermittently at his deepest available level; other parts will resemble slum areas in his own being. Even within simple personality terms, most are aware of hang-ups or hold-ups in their being, of obstinacies they would like to overcome but cannot. Often baffling difficulties are felt to exist, without awareness of their exact source; they are felt by the lacks they bring. These create a prison without walls. Similar hold-ups, as we have seen, can persist in the beyond for many hundreds of years. This is a salutary reminder to endeavour to discover, work through, and dissolve them whilst still on earth.

Sometimes it is comparatively easy to see how people fluctuate between their different selves, as with Elgar, who spoke of *The Dream of Gerontius* as coming from his 'innermost innermost', yet who in another part of his personality continued to be occupied for many years with time-wasting japes and ploys.

So parts of people get left behind; parts which a compassionate psychologist has described as lost children within the psyche. Many men and women are self-maimed, incomplete beings who take this wounded being with them when they die. All are prodigal sons and daughters, even when labouring in the vineyard.

It is very important not to lose heart when one realises that some facets will never be made perfect enough in one lifetime to give any rewarding use. This otherwise disappointing side of life can then be accepted as a very valuable preparation for the following incarnation. What is polished now can come to be of the utmost value in the next life, and possessed then as an apparently ready-made talent. If the polishing is imposed by compulsion of circumstances, if one feels pinned down through an unhappy situation, a frustrating job, or unhappy, seemingly unalterable relationships, the long-term implication is that the area of imprisonment can and should become the area of achievement, even if the achievement sometimes remains a private one. Gradually, through life after life, the personality learns to be obedient to the soul, the horse to the rider, the servant to the over-arching purpose he is slowly, so slowly, learning to serve.

Choice souls like the saints by strenuous discipline hasten and bring about before death many experiences which in others only come about after it. Abnegations similar to those which T. E. Lawrence had to face unwillingly in his post-mortem life have been already won through on earth by many more holy and unselfish characters than his. Most of us, unfortunately, allow these unwelcome accostings to wait, postpone them until post-mortem life.

A man cannot stand still. As Jesus said, 'He that is not with me is against me.' When a man fails to respond to the promptings to accomplish the task he has brought down with him, then further accretions will come upon him, and through him upon the world. Then he will play a part in slowing down the general momentum of earth advancement.

11

As familiarity with the inner worlds grows, the way becomes increasingly open by self-training to listen to the voice of the silence. This picturesque phrase refers to the silence in one's inner mind when the perturbations and concerns of the outer self are temporarily stilled. Then it will be found how real this inner shared life can be; how much the companions of the spirit are almost part of oneself, reflecting one's own mind as well as theirs, for there is basic harmony between the two. Sometimes it is easier to listen to the companion than to oneself. Here, areas of the soul world are reaching down to interpenetrate the soul of the one on earth.

In terms of spirit, there is all the time in the world for the development and spiritualising of mankind to come about. In terms of earth, a speeding up of individual consciousness in this century is vitally necessary. It becomes extremely urgent to overcome the retardments brought about by many generations of selfish, materialistic thought and action. The consequences threaten man on every side with pollution, economic chaos and atomic destruction. It is necessary to learn to respond to the more speedy spiritual pace seemingly now planned for – planning which is the fruit of beings in the higher worlds whose intentions gradually percolate through to minds on earth.

Oliver Lodge, after his death, has emphatically declared:

> We have split up life into two parts far too drastically. We have drawn a line, and we must gradually erase that line. We have talked about the spiritual life, and the earth life or the physical life. The two are one and we must make them one again. There is no line, there is no line at all. Man has drawn a line and it must be erased, and it will take some time to erase it completely, but we must work towards that. We must do that in the same way that we must erase – shall we call it? national boundaries, national boundaries and limitations, racial ones. All these must go, and expecially the boundary that we have, quite unnecessarily, erected between what we now call our two worlds, which are one. It is only one world. There is only one world and we must take down these . . . barriers of illusion that compelled us to think there must be two, because through our limitations and ignorance we are unable to look over the self-erected barrier, or to look through it. It must come down. It is your work, it is our work.[5]

This is the most important of all the implications of survival: that the spiritual task which lies before men and women on earth and those who have passed through death is a shared and common one, and not separate and distinct. Parts of it have to be performed individually and parts in collaboration. The collaboration is always there, even when not consciously accepted by those on earth. This task is the regeneration of the world by regeneration of the individual, and the bringing to earth of the Kingdom of Heaven which, as Jesus said, is within and awaits there its finding by every man and woman.

References

CHAPTER 1

1 Letter of 4 April 1787
2 Laurens van der Post, *Jung and the Story of our Time* (Hogarth Press), p. 209
3 Geraldine Cummins, *Swan on a Black Sea* (Routledge), p. 58
4 id., pp. 140–3

CHAPTER 2

1 See, among numerous others, *Survival of Death* by the present author

CHAPTER 4

1 Dr Raymond A. Moody, *Life after Life* (Mockingbird Books, USA), pp. 52–3
2 G. N. M. Tyrrell, *The Personality of Man* (Pelican), pp. 197–8
3 F. S. Smythe, *The Spirit of the Hills* (Hodder & Stoughton, 1937), pp. 277–8. I am indebted to Dr Raynor Johnson for introducing me to this quotation. A number of similar experiences have been gathered together in Russell Noyes Jr and Ray Kletti, *The Experience of Dying from Falls* (Omega, 1972), vol. 3.
4 Chapter by the Revd Donald J. Bretherton in Canon J. D. Pearce-Higgins and the Revd G. Stanley Whitby (eds), *Life, Death and Psychical Research* (Rider), p. 124
5 id., pp. 110–11
6 Baron von Hugel, *The Mystical Element of Religion* (Dent), vol. 1, p. 177
7 id., vol. 2, pp. 46–7
8 See in particular vol. 1, pp. 175–200 and vol. 2, pp. 22–61
9 Chancellor the Revd. E. Garth Moor, *Believe it or not: Christianity and Psychical Research* (Mowbray, 1977), pp. 113–4
10 Revd Harold Anson, *The Truth about Spiritualism* (Student Christian Movement Press, 1941), p. 59
11 A. F. Webling, *Something Beyond* (C.U.P.), p. 271
12 Revd G. Vale Owen, *The Life Beyond the Veil* (Thornton Butterworth), pp. 8–9

13 *Spirit Teachings: M. A. Oxon* (through the mediumship of William Stainton Moses) (C.P.S.), pp. 5–7
14 Geraldine Cummins, op. cit., pp. 160–3 and 168
15 id., p. 25
16 Stewart Edward White, *The Betty Book* (Psychic Press) vol. 1. p. 17
17 id., p. 19
18 A Group of Philosophers, *A New Approach to Metaphysics* (privately printed)

CHAPTER 5

1 John Scott, *As One Ghost to Another* (Psychic Press), p. 108
2 Geraldine Cummins, *The Road to Immortality* (Psychic Press), p. 78
3 Cynthia Sandys and Rosamund Lehmann, *The Awakening Letters* (Neville Spearman), pp. 99–100
4 W. Tudor Pole, Private Dowding (Neville Spearman), pp. 83–90
5 Geraldine Cummins, *Swan on a Black Sea*, p. 139
6 E. Bozzano, *Discarnate Influence in Human Life* (J. M. Watkins and International Institute for Psychical Research), p. 177
7 id., p. 179
8 Revd C. Drayton Thomas, *In the Dawn Beyond Death* (Psychic Press), pp. 12–13
9 Geraldine Cummins, *They Survive* (Psychic Press), p. 49
10 'Joe's Scripts', *Light* (College of Psychic Studies), summer 1970, p. 89
11 Helen Greaves, *Testimony of Light* (Neville Spearman), p. 28
12 John Scott, op. cit., pp. 32–3
13 'Joe's Scripts', p. 88
14 Revd C. Drayton Thomas, *Life Beyond Death with Evidence* (Collins), p. 60
15 ibid.
16 Geraldine Cummins, *Swan on a Black Sea*, p. 139
17 Geraldine Cummins, *The Road to Immortality*, p. 61
18 Geraldine Cummins, *Swan on a Black Sea*, p. 139
19 id., p. 144

CHAPTER 6

1 'Joe's Scripts', pp. 87–90
2 paraphrased from the Hunt Tapes
3 Armido, *The Wisdom of the Spirit* (Amica) pp. 94–6
4 *Trance Talks by Chan, Guide of Ivy Northage* (S.A.G.B.), p. 32
5 Dr Raynor Johnson, *Watcher on the Hills* (Hodder & Stoughton), p. 61
6 Dr Robert Crookall, *The Interpretation of Cosmic and Mystical Experiences* (James Clarke & Co.), p. 20 (quoting from the *Journal* of the American Society for Psychical Research)
7 Cynthia Sandys and Rosamund Lehmann, *The Awakening Letters* (Neville Spearman), p. 23

8 Jane Sherwood, *Post-mortem Journal* (Neville Spearman), p. 26
9 A. Pauchard, 'The Other World', Paper 7 (College of Psychic Studies), pp. 15–16
10 Geraldine Cummins, *The Road to Immortality*, p. 49
11 A. Pauchard, op. cit., pp. 38–9
12 Dr Margaret Vivian, *The Doorway* (Psychic Press), p. 49
13 Revd A. W. Jackson, *The Celtic Church Speaks Today?* (World Fellowship Press)
14 Helen Greaves, op. cit., pp. 97–8
15 Dr Sherwood Eddy, *You Will Survive Death* (Omega Press) pp. 136–9
16 *Trance Talks by Chan*, p. 27
17 Jasper Swain, *On the Death of My Son* (Turnstone Books), p. 36
18 Harry Dodd, *An Artist's Experiences after Death* (printed by his widow), p. 11

CHAPTER 7

1 Pardoe Woodman and Estelle Stead, *The Blue Island* (Hutchinson), p. 133
2 Rudolf Steiner, *The Theosophy of the Rosicrucians* (Rudolf Steiner Publishing Co.), pp. 33–4
3 *Trance Talks by Chan*, p. 16
4 A. Pauchard, op. cit., pp. 9–10
5 id., pp. 10–11
6 Jane Sherwood, op. cit., pp. 35–6
7 A. Pauchard, op. cit., p. 55

CHAPTER 8

1 Anonymous young artist, *The Bridge Over the River* (The Anthroposophic Press, N.Y.), p. 58
2 A. Pauchard, op. cit., p. 136
3 F. Bligh Bond, *The Gate of Remembrance* (Blackwell), p. 100
4 John H. Remmers, *The Great Reality* (Spiritualist Press), pp. 123–5
5 Woodman and Stead, op. cit., p. 133
6 Lady Barrett, *Personality Survives Death* (Longman), pp. 159–61
7 Paul Beard, 'The James–John Experiment', Paper 6 (College of Psychic Studies), pp. 30–1
8 Erik Palmstierna, *Horizons of Immortality* (Constable), pp. 347–50
9 Erik Palmstierna, *Widening Horizons* (John Lane, The Bodley Head) pp. 249–50
10 Jane Sherwood, op. cit., pp. 31–3
11 Revd Charles Fryer, *A Hand in Dialogue* (manuscript version), p. 148
12 Revd C. Drayton Thomas, *Beyond Life's Sunset* (Psychic Press), p. 12
13 id., p. 16
14 Geraldine Cummins, *The Road to Immortality*, p. 55
15 Woodman and Stead, op. cit., p. 142
16 Private discarnate teaching

CHAPTER 9

1 *The Bridge Over the River*, p. 34
2 Sherwood Eddy, op. cit., p. 128
3 Geraldine Cummins, *The Road to Immortality*, p. 66
4 Woodman and Stead, op. cit., p. 149
5 Sherwood Eddy, op. cit., p. 134
6 Privately distributed teaching (White Eagle Lodge)
7 Ivan Cooke, *Thy Kingdom Come* (White Eagle Publishing Trust), p. 163
8 Harry Dodd, op. cit., pp. 16–17

CHAPTER 10

1 *Trance Talks by Chan*, pp. 9–10
2 Geraldine Cummins, *The Road to Immortality*, p. 67
3 *The Rosicrucian Cosmo-Conception*, p. 122
4 Veronica, *Co-operation* (Arthur H. Stockwell), pp. 219–21
5 Helen Greaves, op. cit., p. 111
6 Pauchard, op. cit., p. 135
7 Palmstierna, *Horizons of Immortality*, p. 168
8 Pauchard, op. cit., pp. 136–7
9 Cynthia Lady Sandys and Rosamond Lehmann, 'Letters from our Daughters', Paper 1 (College of Psychic Studies), pp. 25–6
10 Pauchard, op. cit., p. 29
11 Helen Greaves, op. cit., pp. 112–13

CHAPTER 11

1 Lady Barrett, op. cit., pp. 166–71
2 Privately distributed teaching
3 Lady Barrett, op. cit., pp. 166–71
4 Palmstierna, *Horizons of Immortality*, p. 192
5 From an unpublished script
6 Privately distributed teaching (White Eagle Lodge)
7 Laurence Temple, *The Shining Brother* (Psychic Press), pp. 32–4
8 Revd C. Drayton Thomas, *In the Dawn Beyond Death*, pp. 92–4
9 Laurence Temple, op. cit., pp. 66–7
10 id., p. 68
11 Geraldine Cummins, *Swan on a Black Sea*, p. 105
12 id., p. 106

CHAPTER 12

1 Inner teaching (White Eagle Lodge)
2 Geraldine Cummins, *The Road to Immortality*, p. 71

CHAPTER 14

1 Lawrence Hyde, *The Planes of Ascension* (circulated privately)
2 Stewart Edward White, op. cit., pp. 54–5
3 Pauchard, op. cit., p. 24
4 *Journal* of the Society for Psychical Research, June 1945, vol. 33, p. 140
5 id., p. 146

Index